Dart: Up and Running

Kathy Walrath and Seth Ladd

Beijing · Cambridge · Farnham · Köln · Sebastopol · Tokyo

Dart: Up and Running

by Kathy Walrath and Seth Ladd

Copyright © 2014 Kathy Walrath, Seth Ladd. All rights reserved.

Printed in the United States of America.

Published by O'Reilly Media, Inc., 1005 Gravenstein Highway North, Sebastopol, CA 95472.

O'Reilly books may be purchased for educational, business, or sales promotional use. Online editions are also available for most titles (*http://my.safaribooksonline.com*). For more information, contact our corporate/institutional sales department: 800-998-9938 or *corporate@oreilly.com*.

Editor: Meghan Blanchette	**Cover Designer:** Randy Comer
Production Editor: Melanie Yarbrough	**Interior Designer:** David Futato
Proofreader: Melanie Yarbrough	**Illustrator:** Rebecca Demarest

Revision History for the First Edition:

2012-10-24: First release

2013-03-29: Second release

2014-02-19: Third release

See *http://oreilly.com/catalog/errata.csp?isbn=9781449330897* for release details.

ISBN: 978-1-449-33089-7

[LSI]

Table of Contents

Foreword

When we joined Google and entered the fascinating world of web browser development more than six years ago, the web was a different place. It was clear that a new breed of web apps was emerging, but the performance of the underlying platform left much to be desired. Given our background in designing and implementing virtual machines, building a high performance JavaScript engine seemed like an interesting challenge. It was. We implemented the V8 JavaScript engine from scratch and shipped it as part of Google Chrome in 2008, and we are very proud of the positive performance impact our work seems to have had on the entire browser industry.

Even though recent performance gains in web browsers have shattered most limits on how large and complex web apps can be, building large, high-performance web apps remains hard. Without good abstraction mechanisms and clean semantics, developers often end up with complex and convoluted code. Naturally, this problem gets exacerbated as the codebase grows. We designed the Dart programming language to solve this exact problem, and we hope that programmers will be more productive as a result.

It is very satisfying to see how Dart inspires programmers to strive for concise, elegant programs. There is something very enjoyable about incrementally transforming prototypes into maintainable production software through refactorings and adding type annotations—and it definitely feels like Dart as a language scales well from small experiments to large projects with lots of code.

Dart: Up and Running is a practical guide that introduces the Dart programming language and teaches you how to build Dart applications. We hope you will enjoy the book and Dart.

—Lars Bak and Kasper Lund
Designers of the Dart programming language
October 2012

Preface

You don't need to be an expert web developer to build web apps. With Dart, you can be productive as you build high-performance apps for the modern web.

Our aim for this book is to be a useful introduction to the Dart language, libraries, and tools. Because this book is short and Dart is young, you might also need to refer to the Dart website at *http://dartlang.org*—both for details and for updates. For the latest news, keep an eye on the Dart page[1] on Google+.

Another important website is this book's GitHub project.[2] The text for this work is available there under the Creative Commons Attribution-Noncommercial-No Derivative Works 3.0 United States License.[3] Source code files for this book's samples are also there, in the code/ subdirectory.[4] Downloading the sample code from GitHub is much easier than copying it from the book.

If you find an error in the sample code or text, please create an issue.[5]

Conventions Used in This Book

The following typographical conventions are used in this book:

Italic
Indicates new terms, URLs, email addresses, filenames, and file extensions.

---

1. *http://google.com/+dartlang*
2. *https://github.com/dart-lang/dart-up-and-running-book*
3. *http://creativecommons.org/licenses/by-nc-nd/3.0/us/*
4. *https://github.com/dart-lang/dart-up-and-running-book/tree/master/code*
5. *https://github.com/dart-lang/dart-up-and-running-book/issues/new*

`Constant width`
> Used for program listings, as well as within paragraphs to refer to program elements such as variable or function names, databases, data types, environment variables, statements, and keywords.

`Constant width bold`
> Shows commands or other text that should be typed literally by the user.

`Constant width italic`
> Shows text that should be replaced with user-supplied values or by values determined by context.

 This icon signifies a tip or suggestion.

 This icon signifies a general note.

 This icon indicates a warning or caution.

Using Code Examples

Supplemental material (code examples, exercises, etc.) is available for download at *https://github.com/oreillymedia/dart_up_and_running*.

This book is here to help you get your job done. In general, if example code is offered with this book, you may use it in your programs and documentation. You do not need to contact us for permission unless you're reproducing a significant portion of the code. For example, writing a program that uses several chunks of code from this book does not require permission. Selling or distributing a CD-ROM of examples from O'Reilly books does require permission. Answering a question by citing this book and quoting example code does not require permission. Incorporating a significant amount of example code from this book into your product's documentation does require permission.

We appreciate, but do not require, attribution. An attribution usually includes the title, author, publisher, and ISBN. For example: *"Dart: Up and Running by Kathy Walrath and Seth Ladd (O'Reilly). Copyright 2014 Kathy Walrath and Seth Ladd, 978-1-449-33089-7."*

If you feel your use of code examples falls outside fair use or the permission given above, feel free to contact us at *permissions@oreilly.com*.

Safari® Books Online

 Safari Books Online (*www.safaribooksonline.com*) is an on-demand digital library that delivers expert content in both book and video form from the world's leading authors in technology and business.

Technology professionals, software developers, web designers, and business and creative professionals use Safari Books Online as their primary resource for research, problem solving, learning, and certification training.

Safari Books Online offers a range of product mixes and pricing programs for organizations, government agencies, and individuals. Subscribers have access to thousands of books, training videos, and prepublication manuscripts in one fully searchable database from publishers like O'Reilly Media, Prentice Hall Professional, Addison-Wesley Professional, Microsoft Press, Sams, Que, Peachpit Press, Focal Press, Cisco Press, John Wiley & Sons, Syngress, Morgan Kaufmann, IBM Redbooks, Packt, Adobe Press, FT Press, Apress, Manning, New Riders, McGraw-Hill, Jones & Bartlett, Course Technology, and dozens more. For more information about Safari Books Online, please visit us online.

How to Contact Us

Please address comments and questions concerning this book to the publisher:

> O'Reilly Media, Inc.
> 1005 Gravenstein Highway North
> Sebastopol, CA 95472
> 800-998-9938 (in the United States or Canada)
> 707-829-0515 (international or local)
> 707-829-0104 (fax)

We have a web page for this book, where we list errata, examples, and any additional information. You can access this page at *http://oreil.ly/Dart_Up_and_Running*.

To comment or ask technical questions about this book, send email to *bookquestions@oreilly.com*.

For more information about our books, courses, conferences, and news, see our website at *http://www.oreilly.com*.

Find us on Facebook: *http://facebook.com/oreilly*

Follow us on Twitter: *http://twitter.com/oreillymedia*

Watch us on YouTube: *http://www.youtube.com/oreillymedia*

Content Updates

This section gives details about how the book has changed between each of its three printings.

Changes in the Third Printing: February 19, 2014

We've changed the text and examples to reflect these language changes:

- Instance variables can no longer be const. Use static const variables instead.
- The ? operator for testing whether an optional parameter has been set is no longer in the language.
- Keys in map literals no longer need to be strings.
- Dart now has Symbols and symbol literals (#*identifier*): "Symbols" on page 21.
- Function equality testing is easier: "Testing Functions for Equality" on page 26.
- Bitwise operators have higher precedence than they used to.

We've also updated the content to reflect API changes. In dart:core:

- Set's isSubsetOf() method is gone. Instead, use the Set containsAll() method. You can convert any Iterable to a Set using toSet().
- The Collection class is gone, so we've changed the way we talked about sets, lists, and maps in "Collections" on page 65, and we talk more about Iterable.
- The functionality in the former dart:uri library is now in the Uri class in dart:core. The top-level functions encodeUri(), encodeUriComponent(), decodeUri(), and decodeUriComponent() are now static methods in Uri named (respectively) enco deFull(), encodeComponent(), decodeFull(), and decodeComponent(). To create a Uri from a string, you now use the static parse() method. Uri now has a single constructor, which takes the arguments that the Uri.fromComponents() construc-tor used to take. Finally, the domain field is now named host.
- The @deprecated, @override, and @proxy annotations moved from the meta pack-age to dart:core.

In dart:io:

- File's `openWrite()` method now has no required parameters but two optional named parameters. The `mode` parameter has a default value of `FileMode.WRITE`.
- File's `readAsString()` and `readAsLines()` methods no longer require a parameter. Instead, they have an optional named parameter (`encoding`), with a default value of `Encoding.UTF_8`.
- IOSink's methods for writing data have changed. To write string data, instead of `addString()` use `write()`. The method for writing binary data was temporarily renamed to `writeBytes()`, but reverted back to `add()`.

A new dart:convert library replaces dart:json and dart:uri:

- Instead of a StringDecoder, use `UTF8.decoder` to convert UTF-8 characters into a Dart string.
- Instead of a LineTransformer, use a LineSplitter object to split a stream of strings into a stream of individual lines.
- Where you used to use dart:json's top-level `parse()` and `stringify()` functions, use `JSON.decode()` and `JSON.encode()`, respectively.
- Where you used to use dart:uri's top-level `decodeUri()` and `encodeUri()` functions, use `UTF8.decode()` and `UTF8.encode()`, respectively.

Other API changes include:

- In dart:html, the `query()` and `queryAll()` methods changed to `querySelector()` and `querySelectorAll()`, respectively.
- The dart:crypto library moved out of the SDK (to *http://pub.dartlang.org/packages/crypto*).
- The AsyncError class was removed (from dart:async).
- The dart:isolate library was refactored to have only core primitives. We removed its coverage from the book but expect higher level APIs to come along that make using isolates easier.
- The main() function now takes an optional argument (List<String>).

The sections that talk about tools have changed, too:

- The dart_analyzer tool has been replaced by dartanalyzer.
- Command-line arguments for many tools have changed.
- The pub tool now has build and serve commands, which work with transformers to convert your source files into their final format.

- We fleshed out the dart2js docs.
- We removed the dartdoc coverage from the book, since we expect the interface to change significantly.

We also added new coverage of previously undocumented features and tweaked existing coverage. In the language tour:

- Added "Adding Features to a Class: Mixins" on page 49.
- In "Keywords" on page 13, marked which keywords are built-in identifiers and discussed how they differ from reserved words.
- Added coverage of the + operator for strings.
- Discussed using expressions (such as function calls) as arguments to a non-default constructor.
- Added examples of using the @override and @proxy annotations.
- Changed the doc comment example to match the latest guidelines, and pointed to Guidelines for Dart Doc Comments.[6]

In the library tour:

- Added "dart:mirrors—Reflection" on page 98.
- Added examples of parsing non-decimal numbers.
- Removed the incorrect new from the example of using Future.wait().
- Removed coverage of Completer, which is no longer recommended.
- Added "Stream" on page 78.

Throughout the book, we updated links to related topics.

Finally, we completely rewrote Chapter 5 to feature a new example (Dartiverse Search).

Changes in the Second Printing: March 29, 2013

We've updated the content to reflect the following changes since the first printing:

- Using part of in additional library files is now *required*, not optional.
- In M2, several APIs changed:
  - In the dart:html library, the elements property of Element changed to children.
  - Names in dart:html changed to conform to Dart naming standards. In particular, innerHTML became innerHtml.

---

6. *https://www.dartlang.org/articles/doc-comment-guidelines/*

— The charCodes() method of String became a getter, so we removed the parentheses from all references to charCodes.

— The readAsText() method of File became readAsString().

— Constructors for the Date class changed.

— NullPointerException no longer exists.

— RegExp no longer has a const constructor.

— The return type of StringBuffer's add() method changed to void. Code that used to chain calls to add() should now use method cascades instead.

• The recommended way for web apps to use dart.js is now to have a local copy, preferably one downloaded using the browser pub package.

• Metadata support was added to the language. See "Metadata" on page 57.

• We added references to the Web UI package[7], which provides a higher level, scalable approach to creating UIs for web apps.

• In M3, mixins were added to the language, enabling code re-use between classes.

• The core libraries were greatly revised in M3 or shortly afterward. Changes include:

— Some methods changed to fields or getters. This meant we had to remove the () after hashCode, isEmpty, and isNan. We also changed getKeys() to keys, and getValues() to values.

— The Iterable class was beefed up, affecting all Collections such as Lists and Sets. The former Collection methods filter() and map() moved to Iterable, and the name of filter() changed to where(). (map() was briefly renamed to mapped By(), but due to public feedback that decision was reversed.) The some() method changed to any(). Many values returned by Iterables are now lazily-filled Iterables; you can use toList() or toSet() to force evaluation. We recommend *extending* Iterable rather than just implementing it, so you can take advantage of added functionality. More details are in the article Iterables.[8]

— The Iterator interface changed from next() and hasNext() to current and moveNext().

— The dart:json library no longer has a JSON class. Former JSON static methods such as parse() and stringify() are now top-level functions.

— Date is now named DateTime, and the fromString() constructor is now a static method named parse().

— Event-handler registration used to be .on.event.add(); now it's .on*Event*.listen.

7. *http://www.dartlang.org/articles/web-ui/*
8. *http://www.dartlang.org/articles/m3-whats-new/iterables.html*

— The dart:html HttpRequest `get()` method was replaced by `getString()` and `request()`, which return Future<String> and Future<HttpRequest>, respectively.

— The dart:html Window `setTimeout()` method is gone; instead, use `Future.de layed()` or, if you know what you're doing, a Timer.

— Timer and Completer moved from dart:isolate to a new library called dart:async. The Timer constructors now take a Duration instead of an int.

— The Future `chain()` and `handleException()` methods are gone, replaced by `then()` and `catchError()`.

— The String `splitChars()` method is gone; instead, use `split()` with an empty string argument. String's `charCodes` getter and `charCodeAt()` method are gone; to get UTF-16 code units, use String's `codeUnits` or `codeUnitAt()` instead.

— The StringBuffer `add()` and `addAll()` methods were replaced by `write()` and `writeAll()`, respectively.

— The dart:io library changed significantly after M3, as did all I/O in Dart. I/O now centers around the dart:async library's Stream and Future classes, instead of callbacks. The InputStream and OutputStream classes were replaced with classes implementing Stream[9] and IOSink.[10] A new FileSystemEntity[11] class is the superclass of File and Directory. To create a new HttpServer, you now use the static `bind()` method. For more information, see the announcement.[12]

— The most used dart:crypto methods for hashes changed from `update()` and `digest()` to `add()` and `close()`.

We corrected or clarified some text, such as:

- Bitwise operators are implemented in **int**, not num.

- The `is` and `as` examples (in "Type Test Operators" on page 29) aren't completely equivalent.

We also added sections for some pre-existing features:

- Keywords (see "Keywords" on page 13)

- Lexical scope (see "Lexical Scope" on page 25)

- Function equality (see "Testing Functions for Equality" on page 26)

---

9. *http://api.dartlang.org/docs/releases/latest/dart_async/Stream.html*
10. *http://api.dartlang.org/dart_io/IOSink.html*
11. *http://api.dartlang.org/dart_io/FileSystemEntity.html*
12. *http://news.dartlang.org/2013/02/io-library-now-uses-streams.html*

- The dart_analyzer tool (see "dartanalyzer: The Static Analyzer" on page 121)

Finally, Figure 1-1 now uses a more recent benchmark and has the latest numbers.

Acknowledgments

We'd like to thank the many people who contributed to this book. We hope we haven't forgotten anyone, but we probably have.

The following Dart engineers and managers gave us prompt, helpful reviews and information for the sections corresponding to their areas of responsibility: Mads Ager, Peter von der Ahé, Justin Fagnani, Emily Fortuna, Søren Gjesse, Dan Grove, Matthias Hausner, Florian Loitsch, Ryan Macnak, Sam McCall, John McCutchan, Vijay Menon, John Messerly, Anton Muhin, Lasse R.H. Nielsen, Bob Nystrom, Keerti Parthasarathy, Ivan Posva, Konstantin Scheglov, Brian Wilkerson, and Jaime Wren.

We'd especially like to thank the people who reviewed even bigger swaths of the book or contributed in other, large ways:

- JJ Behrens, whose careful look at the first draft of the book helped us catch errors and inconsistencies, as well as rework Chapter 5 to be more interesting, and less of a laundry list. He also created a system for testing our samples.
- Shailen Tuli, who helped test our examples although he didn't even work for Google.
- Mary Campione, whose stream-of-consciousness review of the entire book, performed while she was first learning the language, helped us find and fix many confusing spots, as well as some errors. Later she reviewed and updated our samples, and she implemented continuous build testing for our samples on drone.io.
- Phil Quitslund, who did a big-picture review of the book and gave us guidance and encouragement.
- Kasper Lund, whose review caught issues that only someone with his expert, comprehensive knowledge of the Dart language and libraries could have found.
- Gilad Bracha, the language spec writer whose reviews of the language chapter were invaluable for getting language details right. We couldn't cover everything, so we look forward to his future work on making all the corners of the language understandable to all Dart programmers.
- Anders Johnsen, who wrote the Dartiverse Search app and reviewed Chapter 5's walkthrough of that app.

Other Googlers helped, as well. Vivian Cromwell, the head of Chrome Developer Relations, supported our work on this book. Andres Ferrate, the Google Press liaison to O'Reilly, helped simplify the process of getting the book published. Myisha Harris gave us excellent legal advice.

The people at O'Reilly were extremely helpful. Meghan Blanchette, our editor, kept everything going smoothly, monitoring our progress in the nicest possible way. Christopher Hearse, Marisa LaFleur, and Melanie Yarbrough checked our work and helped us make some last-minute fixes that improved the final result. We'd also like to thank the good people who manage the author workflow and make working on an O'Reilly book such a pleasure. We personally worked with Sarah Schneider, Jessica Hosman, and Rachel James.

Finally, we thank Lars Bak and Kasper Lund for writing the foreword, and most of all for creating Dart.

CHAPTER 1

Quick Start

Welcome to Dart, an open-source, batteries-included developer platform for building structured HTML5 web apps. This chapter tells you why Google created Dart, what's cool about Dart, and how to write and run your first Dart app.

Dart provides not only a new language, but libraries, an editor, a virtual machine (VM), a browser that can run Dart apps natively, and a compiler to JavaScript. Dart aims to be a more productive way to build the high-performance, modern apps that users demand.

Why Google Created Dart

Google cares a lot about helping to make the Web great. We write a lot of web apps, many of them quite sophisticated—think Gmail, Google Calendar, Google+, and more. We want web apps to load quickly, run smoothly, and present engaging and fun experiences to users. We want developers of all backgrounds to be able to build great experiences for the browser.

As an example of Google's commitment to the Web, consider the Google Chrome browser. Google created it to spur competition at a time when the web platform seemed to be stagnating. It worked. As Figure 1-1 shows, browser speed has increased immensely since Chrome's introduction in 2008.

 The JavaScript engine known as *V8* is responsible for much of Chrome's speed. Many of the V8 engineers are now working on the Dart project.

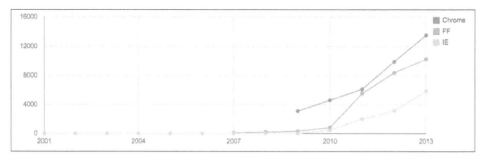

Figure 1-1. Browser speed (V8 benchmark suite v7; higher numbers are better)

The number of new features in browsers has also increased, with APIs such as WebGL, FileSystem, Web workers, and WebSockets. Browsers now have automatic update capabilities, frequently delivering new features and fixes directly to the user. Mobile devices such as tablets and phones also have modern browsers with many HTML5 features.

Despite these improvements in the web platform, the developer experience hasn't improved as much as we'd like. We believe it should be easier to build larger, more complex web apps. It's taken far too long for productive tools to emerge, and they still don't match the capabilities offered by other developer platforms. You shouldn't have to be intimately familiar with web programming to start building great apps for the modern web. And even though JavaScript engines are getting faster, web apps still start up much too slowly.

We expect Dart to help in two main ways:

Better performance
> As VM engineers, the designers of Dart know how to build a language for performance. A more structured language is easier to optimize, and a fresh VM enables improvements such as faster startup.

Better productivity
> Support for libraries and packages helps you work with other developers and easily reuse code from other projects. Types can make APIs clearer and easier to use. Tools help you refactor, navigate, and debug code.

A Quick Look at the Dart Language

It's hard to talk about a language without seeing it. Here's a peek at a small Dart program:

```
import 'dart:math';

class Point {
  num x, y;
  Point(this.x, this.y);
  num distanceTo(Point other) {
    var dx = x - other.x;
    var dy = y - other.y;
    return sqrt(dx * dx + dy * dy);
  }
}

main() {
  var p = new Point(2, 3);
  var q = new Point(3, 4);
  print('distance from p to q = ${p.distanceTo(q)}');
}
```

Of course, Dart's main use case is building modern web apps. Programming the browser is easy:

```
import 'dart:html';

main() {
  var button = new ButtonElement();
  button..id = 'confirm'
        ..text = 'Click to Confirm'
        ..classes.add('important')
        ..onClick.listen((e) => window.alert('Confirmed!'));
  querySelector('#registration').children.add(button);
}
```

You'll learn about the Dart language and libraries in Chapters 2 and 3, respectively.

What's Cool About Dart

Dart may look familiar, but don't let that fool you. Dart has lots of cool features to help give you a productive and fun experience building the next generation of awesome web apps.

Dart is easy to learn. A wide range of developers can learn Dart quickly. It's an object-oriented language with classes, single inheritance, lexical scope, top-level functions, and a familiar syntax. Most developers are up and running with Dart in just a few hours.

Dart compiles to JavaScript. Dart has been designed from the start to compile to Java-Script, so that Dart apps can run across the entire modern web. Every feature considered for the language must somehow be translated to performant and logical JavaScript before it is added. Dart draws a line in the sand and doesn't support older, legacy browsers.

Dart runs in the client and on the server. The Dart virtual machine (VM) can be integrated into a web browser, but it can also run standalone on the command line. With built-in library support for files, directories, sockets, and even web servers, you can use Dart for full end-to-end apps.

Dart comes with a lightweight editor. You can use Dart Editor to write, launch, and debug Dart apps. The editor can help you with code completion, detecting potential bugs, debugging both command-line and web apps, and even refactoring. Dart Editor isn't required for writing Dart; it's just a tool that can help you write better code faster.

Dart supports types, without requiring them. You can omit types when you want to move very quickly, aren't sure what structure to take, or simply want to express something you can't with the type system. You can add types as your program matures, the structure becomes more evident, and more developers join the project. Dart's optional types are static type annotations that act as documentation, clearly expressing your intent. Using types means that fewer comments are required to document the code, and tools can give better warnings and error messages.

Dart scales from small scripts to large, complex apps. Web development is very much an iterative process. With the reload button acting as your compiler, building the seed of a web app is often a fun experience of writing a few functions just to experiment. As the idea grows, you can add more code and structure. Thanks to Dart's support for top-level functions, optional types, classes, and libraries, your Dart programs can start small and grow over time. Tools such as Dart Editor help you refactor and navigate your code as it evolves.

Dart has a wide array of built-in libraries. The core library supports built-in types and other fundamental features such as collections, dates, and regular expressions. Web apps can use the HTML library—think DOM programming, but optimized for Dart. Command-line apps can use the I/O library to work with files, directories, sockets, and servers. Other libraries include URI, UTF, Crypto, Math, and Unit test.

Dart supports safe, simple concurrency with isolates. Traditional shared-memory threads are difficult to debug and can lead to deadlocks. Dart's isolates, inspired by Erlang, provide an easier to understand model for running isolated, but concurrent, portions of your code. Spawning new isolates is cheap and fast, and no state is shared.

Dart supports code sharing. Traditional web programming workflows can't integrate third-party libraries from arbitrary sources or frameworks. With the Dart package manager (pub) and language features such as libraries, you can easily discover, install, and integrate code from across the Web and enterprise.

Dart is open source. Dart was born for the Web, and it's available under a BSD-style license. You can find the project's issue tracker and source repository[1] online. Maybe you'll submit the next patch?

Up and Running

Now that you know something about Dart, get ready to code! These instructions feature the open-source Dart Editor tool. When you download Dart, you not only get Dart Editor, but also tools such as the Dart-to-JavaScript compiler and a version of Chromium (nicknamed *Dartium*) that includes the Dart VM.

 If you run into trouble installing and using Dart Editor, see Troubleshooting Dart Editor.[2]

Step 1: Download and Install the Software

In this step, you'll install Dart Editor and, if necessary, a Java runtime environment. (To avoid having to modify the PATH environment variable, you can install the JRE under your Dart installation directory, in a subdirectory named `jre`.)

1. Download Dart[3].
2. Unarchive the file you downloaded. The resulting directory, which we'll call your *Dart installation directory*, contains the `DartEditor` executable and several subdirectories.
3. If you don't already have a Java runtime, download and install it. Dart Editor requires Java version 6 or higher.

Step 2: Launch the Editor

Go to your Dart installation directory, and double-click the **DartEditor** executable 🔍.

You should see the Dart Editor application window appear, looking something like Figure 1-2.

---

1. *http://dart.googlecode.com*
2. *http://www.dartlang.org/tools/editor/troubleshoot.html*
3. *http://dartlang.org/#get-started*

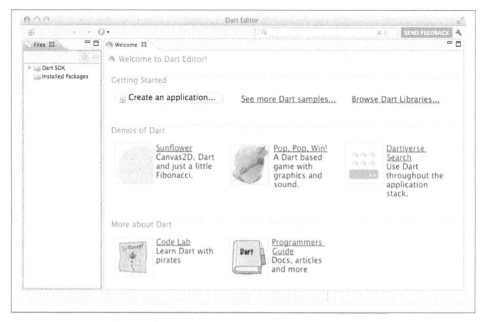

Figure 1-2. Dart Editor and its Welcome page

Step 3: Open and Run a Demo

The Dart Editor bundle comes with several demos and samples. In this step, you'll open a web app and run it in Dartium:

1. Click the **Welcome** tab. Or choose **Welcome Page** from the **Tools** menu.

2. In the Welcome tab, click the image labeled **Sunflower**. Dart Editor creates a copy of the Sunflower app's directory,[4] and the Editor view displays the contents of *web/sunflower.dart*.

3. Click the Run button ⊙. Dart Editor launches Dartium, which displays *sunflower.html*.

Dartium is a technical preview, and it might have security and stability issues. *Do not use Dartium as your primary browser!*

4. Move the slider to change the sunflower's display, as shown in Figure 1-3.

---

4. *http://code.google.com/p/dart/source/browse/trunk/dart/samples/sunflower/*

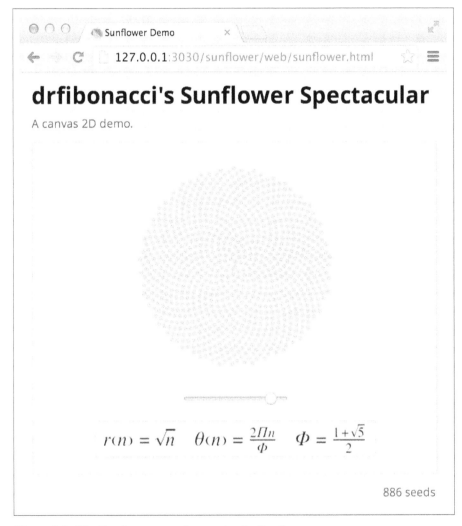

Figure 1-3. The Sunflower sample running in Dartium

Step 4: Create and Run an App

It's easy to create a simple web or command-line app from scratch. This step walks you through creating and running a command-line app:

1. Click the New Application button ⊞ (at the upper-left of Dart Editor). Alternatively, choose **File→New Application** from the Dart Editor menu, or click the **Create an Application...** button in the Welcome page. A dialog appears (see Figure 1-4).

2. Type in a name for your application—for example, hello_world. If you don't like the default directory, type in a new location or browse to choose the location.

3. Make sure **Generate sample content** and **Command-line application** are selected. Then click **Finish** to create the initial files for the app.

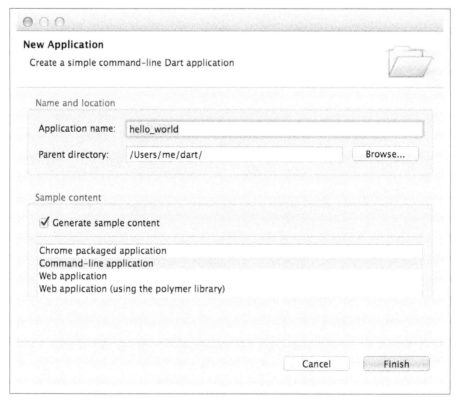

Figure 1-4. Create command-line or web apps with Dart Editor

A default Dart file appears in the Edit view, and its directory appears in the Files view. Your Dart Editor window should look something like Figure 1-5.

4. Click the Run button ⊚ to run your new app.

For command-line apps, the output of print() appears at the bottom-right, in a new tab next to the Problems tab.

What Next?

Now that you know the basics, you can learn more about Dart Editor and help improve it.

Figure 1-5. Dart Editor displaying a new app's files

Follow a code lab

Go to *http://dartlang.org/codelabs* to find the latest step-by-step instructions for writing an app. The first code lab, Try Dart,[5] guides you through using Dart Editor to build and run a pirate name badge generator.

Read tutorials

The Dart Tutorials[6] teach you how to build web applications using the Dart language, tools, and APIs.

Become a power user

Visit the Dart Editor homepage[7] for help on using Dart Editor's expanding feature set.

Send feedback

Click the **SEND FEEDBACK** link (at the upper-right of the Dart Editor window) whenever you notice a problem or have an idea for improving Dart Editor. We'll open a new issue for you, if appropriate, without disclosing your sensitive or personally identifiable information.

---

5. *https://www.dartlang.org/codelabs/darrrt/*

6. *http://www.dartlang.org/docs/tutorials/*

7. *http://www.dartlang.org/editor/*

CHAPTER 2

A Tour of the Dart Language

This chapter shows you how to use each major Dart feature, from variables and operators to classes and libraries, with the assumption that you already know how to program in another language.

> To play with each feature, create a command-line application project in Dart Editor, as described in "Up and Running" on page 5.

Consult the Dart Language Specification[1] whenever you want more details about a language feature.

A Basic Dart Program

The following code uses many of Dart's most basic features:

```
// Define a function.
printNumber(num aNumber) {
  print('The number is $aNumber.'); // Print to the console.
}

// This is where the app starts executing.
main() {
  var number = 42;          // Declare and initialize a variable.
  printNumber(number);      // Call a function.
}
```

Here's what this program uses that applies to all (or almost all) Dart apps:

---

1. *http://www.dartlang.org/docs/spec/*

```
// This is a comment.
```
Use // to indicate that the rest of the line is a comment. Alternatively, use /* ... */. For details, see "Comments" on page 58.

`num`
> A type. Some of the other built-in types are String, int, and bool.

`42`
> A number *literal*. Literals are a kind of compile-time constant.

`print()`
> A handy way to display output.

`'...' (or "...")`
> A string literal.

`$variableName (or ${expression})`
> String interpolation, including a variable or expression's string equivalent inside of a string literal. For more information, see "Strings" on page 17.

`main()`
> The special *required* top-level function where app execution starts. For more information, see "The main() Function" on page 24.

`var`
> A way to declare a variable without specifying its type.

 Our code follows the conventions in the Dart Style Guide.[2] For example, we use two-space indentation.

Important Concepts

As you learn about the Dart language, keep these facts and concepts in mind:

- Everything you can place in a variable is an *object*, and every object is an instance of a *class*. Even numbers, functions, and null are objects. All objects inherit from the Object[3] class.

- Specifying static types (such as num in the preceding example) clarifies your intent and enables static checking by tools, but it's optional. (You might notice when you're

2. *http://www.dartlang.org/articles/style-guide/*
3. *http://api.dartlang.org/dart_core/Object.html*

debugging your code that variables with no specified type get a special type: dynamic.)

- Dart parses all your code before running it. You can provide tips to Dart—for example, by using types or compile-time constants—to catch errors or help your code run faster.

- Dart supports top-level functions (such as main( )), as well as functions tied to a class or object (*static* and *instance methods*, respectively). You can also create functions within functions (*nested* or *local functions*).

- Similarly, Dart supports top-level *variables*, as well as variables tied to a class or object (static and instance variables). Instance variables are sometimes known as *fields* or *properties*.

- Unlike Java, Dart doesn't have the keywords public, protected, and private. If an identifier starts with an underscore (_), it's private to its library. For details, see "Libraries and Visibility" on page 53.

- *Identifiers* can start with a letter or _, followed by any combination of those characters plus digits.

- Sometimes it matters whether something is an *expression* or a *statement*, so we'll be precise about those two words.

- Dart tools can report two kinds of problems: warnings and errors. Warnings are just indications that your code might not work, but they don't prevent your program from executing. Errors can be either compile-time or runtime. A compile-time error prevents the code from executing at all; a runtime error results in an exception (page 36) being raised while the code executes.

- Dart has two *runtime modes*: production and checked. Production is faster, but checked is helpful at development.

Keywords

Table 2-1 lists the words that the Dart language treats specially.

Table 2-1. Dart keywords

abstract *	continue	extends	implements *	part *	throw
as *	default	factory *	import *	rethrow	true
assert	do	false	in	return	try
break	dynamic *	final	is	set *	typedef *
case	else	finally	library *	static *	var
catch	enum	for	new	super	void
class	export *	get *	null	switch	while

const	external *	if	operator *	this	with

In the keyword table, words with an asterisk (*) are *built-in identifiers*. Although you should generally treat built-in identifiers like reserved words, the only real restriction is that you can't use a built-in identifier as the name of a class or type. Having built-in identifiers enables easier porting from JavaScript to Dart. For example, say some Java-Script code has a variable named `factory`; you don't have to rename it when you port the code to Dart.

Runtime Modes

We recommend that you develop and debug in checked mode, and deploy to production mode.

Production mode is the default runtime mode of a Dart program, optimized for speed. Production mode ignores assert statements (page 36) and static types.

Checked mode is a developer-friendly mode that helps you catch some type errors during runtime. For example, if you assign a non-number to a variable declared as a `num`, then checked mode throws an exception.

Variables

Here's an example of creating a variable and assigning a value to it:

```
var name = 'Bob';
```

Variables are references. The variable called `name` contains a reference to a String object with a value of "Bob".

Default Value

Uninitialized variables have an initial value of `null`. Even variables with numeric types are initially null because numbers are objects:

```
int lineCount;
assert(lineCount == null);
// Variables (even if they will be numbers) are initially null.
```

 The assert() call is ignored in production mode. In checked mode, assert(*condition*) throws an exception unless *condition* is true. For details, see "Assert" on page 36.

Optional Types

You have the option of adding static types to your variable declarations:

```
String name = 'Bob';
```

Adding types is a way to clearly express your intent. Tools such as compilers and editors can use these types to help you, by providing code completion and early warnings for bugs and code completion.

This chapter follows the style guide recommendation[4] of using var, rather than type annotations, for local variables.

Final and Const

If you never intend to change a variable, use final or const, either instead of var or in addition to a type. A final variable can be set only once; a const variable is a compile-time constant.

A local, top-level, or class variable that's declared as final is initialized the first time it's used:

```
final name = 'Bob';    // Or: final String name = 'Bob';
// name = 'Alice';     // Uncommenting this results in an error
```

Lazy initialization of final variables helps apps start up faster.

Use const for variables that you want to be compile-time constants. If the const variable is at the class level, mark it **static const**. (Instance variables can't be const.) Where you declare the variable, set the value to a compile-time constant such as a literal, a const variable, or the result of an arithmetic operation on constant numbers:

```
const bar = 1000000;      // Unit of pressure (in dynes/cm2)
const atm = 1.01325 * bar; // Standard atmosphere
```

Built-in Types

The Dart language has special support for the following types:

---

4. *http://www.dartlang.org/articles/style-guide/#type-annotations*

- numbers
- strings
- booleans
- lists (also known as *arrays*)
- maps
- symbols

You can initialize an object of any of these special types using a literal. For example, `'this is a string'` is a string literal, and `true` is a boolean literal.

Because every variable in Dart refers to an object—an instance of a *class*—you can usually use *constructors* to initialize variables. Some of the built-in types have their own constructors. For example, you can use the `Map()` constructor to create a map, using code such as `new Map()`.

Numbers

Dart numbers come in two flavors:

`int` [5]

Integer values, which generally should be in the range -2^{53} to 2^{53}

`double` [6]

64-bit (double-precision) floating-point numbers, as specified by the IEEE 754 standard

Both `int` and `double` are subtypes of `num`.[7] The num type includes basic operators such as +, -, /, and *, as well as bitwise operators such as >>. The num type is also where you'll find `abs()`, `ceil()`, and `floor()`, among other methods. If num and its subtypes don't have what you're looking for, the Math[8] library might.

 Integers outside of the -2^{53} to 2^{53} range currently behave differently in JavaScript produced from Dart code than they do when the same Dart code runs in the Dart VM. The reason is that Dart is specified to have arbitrary-precision integers, but JavaScript isn't. See issue 1533[9] for details.

---

5. *http://api.dartlang.org/dart_core/int.html*

6. *http://api.dartlang.org/dart_core/double.html*

7. *http://api.dartlang.org/dart_core/num.html*

8. *http://api.dartlang.org/dart_math.html*

9. *http://dartbug.com/1533*

Integers are numbers without a decimal point. Here are some examples of defining integer literals:

```
var x = 1;
var hex = 0xDEADBEEF;
var bigInt = 34653465834652437659238476592374958739845729475934702943870934934347;
```

If a number includes a decimal, it is a double. Here are some examples of defining double literals:

```
var y = 1.1;
var exponents = 1.42e5;
```

Here's how you turn a string into a number, or vice versa:

```
// String -> int
var one = int.parse('1');
assert(one == 1);

// String -> double
var onePointOne = double.parse('1.1');
assert(onePointOne == 1.1);

// int -> String
String oneAsString = 1.toString();
assert(oneAsString == '1');

// double -> String
String piAsString = 3.14159.toStringAsFixed(2);
assert(piAsString == '3.14');
```

The int type specifies the traditional bitwise shift (<<, >>), AND (&), and OR (|) operators. For example:

```
assert((3 << 1) == 6);  // 0011 << 1 == 0110
assert((3 >> 1) == 1);  // 0011 >> 1 == 0001
assert((3 | 4)  == 7);  // 0011 | 0100 == 0111
```

Strings

A Dart string is a sequence of UTF-16 code units. You can use either single or double quotes to create a string:

```
var s1 = 'Single quotes work well for string literals.';
var s2 = "Double quotes work just as well.";
var s3 = 'It\'s easy to escape the string delimiter.';
var s4 = "It's even easier to just use the other string delimiter.";
```

You can put the value of an expression inside a string by using ${*expression*}. If the expression is an identifier, you can skip the {}. To get the string corresponding to an object, Dart calls the object's toString() method:

```
var s = 'string interpolation';

assert('Dart has $s, which is very handy.' ==
       'Dart has string interpolation, which is very handy.');
assert('That deserves all caps. ${s.toUpperCase()} is very handy!' ==
       'That deserves all caps. STRING INTERPOLATION is very handy!');
```

 The == operator tests whether two objects are equivalent. Two strings are equivalent if they contain the same sequence of code units.

You can concatenate strings using adjacent string literals or the + operator:

```
var s1 = 'String ' 'concatenation'
         " works even over line breaks.";
assert(s1 == 'String concatenation works even over line breaks.');

var s2 = 'The addition operator '
         + 'works, as well.';
assert(s2 == 'The addition operator works, as well.');
```

Another way to create a multi-line string: use a triple quote with either single or double quotation marks:

```
var s1 = '''
You can create
multi-line strings like this one.
''';

var s2 = """This is also a
multi-line string.""";
```

You can create a "raw" string by prefixing it with r:

```
var s = r"In a raw string, even \n isn't special.";
```

You can use Unicode escapes inside of strings:

```
print('Unicode escapes work: \u2665'); // Unicode escapes work: [heart]
```

For more information on using strings, see "Strings and Regular Expressions" on page 62.

Booleans

To represent boolean values, Dart has a type named bool. Only two objects have type bool: the boolean literals, true and false.

When Dart expects a boolean value, only the value `true` is treated as true. All other values are treated as false. Unlike in JavaScript, values such as `1`, `"aString"`, and `some Object` are all treated as false.

For example, consider the following code, which is valid both as JavaScript and as Dart code:

```
var name = 'Bob';
if (name) {
  print('You have a name!'); // Prints in JavaScript, not in Dart.
}
```

If you run this code as JavaScript, it prints "You have a name!" because `name` is a non-null object. However, in Dart running in *production mode*, the preceding doesn't print at all because `name` is converted to `false` (because `name != true`). In Dart running in *checked mode*, the previous code throws an exception because the `name` variable is not a bool.

Here's another example of code that behaves differently in JavaScript and Dart:

```
if (1) {
  print('JavaScript prints this line because it thinks 1 is true.');
} else {
  print('Dart in production mode prints this line.');
  // However, in checked mode, if (1) throws an exception.
}
```

> The previous two samples work only in production mode, not checked mode. In checked mode, an exception is thrown if a non-boolean is used when a boolean value is expected.

Dart's treatment of booleans is designed to avoid the strange behaviors that can arise when many values can be treated as true. What this means for you is that, instead of using code like `if (nonbooleanValue)`, you should instead explicitly check for values. For example:

```
// Check for an empty string.
var fullName = '';
assert(fullName.isEmpty);

// Check for zero.
var hitPoints = 0;
assert(hitPoints <= 0);

// Check for null.
var unicorn;
assert(unicorn == null);
```

```
// Check for NaN.
var iMeantToDoThis = 0/0;
assert(iMeantToDoThis.isNaN);
```

Lists

Perhaps the most common collection in nearly every programming language is the *array*, or ordered group of objects. In Dart, arrays are List[10] objects, so we usually just call them *lists*.

Dart list literals look like JavaScript array literals. Here's a simple Dart list:

```
var list = [1,2,3];
```

Lists use zero-based indexing, where 0 is the index of the first element and `list.length` - 1 is the index of the last element. You can get a list's length and refer to list elements just as you would in JavaScript:

```
var list = [1,2,3];
assert(list.length == 3);
assert(list[1] == 2);
```

The List type has many handy methods for manipulating lists. For more information about lists, see "Generics" on page 51 and "Collections" on page 65.

Maps

In general, a map is an object that associates keys and values. Both keys and values can be any type of object. Each *key* occurs only once, but you can use the same *value* multiple times. Dart support for maps is provided by map literals and the Map[11] type.

Here are a couple of simple Dart maps, created using map literals:

```
var gifts = {
// Keys        Values
  'first'  : 'partridge',
  'second' : 'turtledoves',
  'fifth'  : 'golden rings'
};

var nobleGases = {
// Keys  Values
  2  : 'helium',
  10 : 'neon',
  18 : 'argon',
};
```

---

10. *http://api.dartlang.org/dart_core/List.html*

11. *http://api.dartlang.org/dart_core/Map.html*

You can create the same objects using a Map constructor:

```
var gifts = new Map();
gifts['first'] = 'partridge';
gifts['second'] = 'turtledoves';
gifts['fifth'] = 'golden rings';

var nobleGases = new Map();
nobleGases[2] = 'helium';
nobleGases[10] = 'neon';
nobleGases[18] = 'argon';
```

Add a new key-value pair to an existing map just as you would in JavaScript:

```
var gifts = { 'first': 'partridge' };
gifts['fourth'] = 'calling birds';    // Add a key-value pair
```

Retrieve a value from a map the same way you would in JavaScript:

```
var gifts = { 'first': 'partridge' };
assert(gifts['first'] == 'partridge');
```

If you look for a key that isn't in a map, you get a null in return:

```
var gifts = { 'first': 'partridge' };
assert(gifts['fifth'] == null);
```

Use .length to get the number of key-value pairs in the map:

```
var gifts = { 'first': 'partridge' };
gifts['fourth'] = 'calling birds';
assert(gifts.length == 2);
```

For more information about maps, see "Generics" on page 51 and "Maps" on page 68.

Symbols

A Symbol[12] object represents an operator or identifier declared in a Dart program. You might never need to use symbols, but they're invaluable for APIs that refer to identifiers by name, because minification changes identifier names but not identifier symbols.

To get the symbol for an identifier, use a symbol literal, which is just # followed by the identifier:

```
#radix  // The symbol literal for an identifier named 'radix'.
#bar    // The symbol literal for an identifier named 'bar'.
```

For more information on symbols, see "dart:mirrors—Reflection" on page 98.

---

12. *http://api.dartlang.org/dart_core/Symbol.html*

Functions

Here's an example of implementing a function:

```dart
void printNumber(num number) {
  print('The number is $number.');
}
```

Although the style guide recommends specifying the parameter and return types, you don't have to:

```dart
printNumber(number) {          // Omitting types is OK.
  print('The number is $number.');
}
```

For functions that contain just one expression, you can use a shorthand syntax:

```dart
printNumber(number) => print('The number is $number.');
```

The => *expr*; syntax is a shorthand for { return *expr*;}. In the printNumber() function earlier, the expression is the call to the top-level print() function.

 Only an *expression*—not a *statement*—can appear between the arrow (=>) and the semicolon (;). For example, you can't put an if statement (page 32) there, but you can use a conditional (?:) expression (page 32).

You can use types with =>, although the convention is not to do so:

```dart
printNumber(num number) => print('The number is $number.'); // Types are OK.
```

Here's an example of calling a function:

```dart
printNumber(123);
```

A function can have two types of parameters: required and optional. The required parameters are listed first, followed by any optional parameters.

Optional Parameters

Optional parameters can be either positional or named, but not both.

Both kinds of optional parameter can have default values. The default values must be compile-time constants such as literals. If no default value is provided, the value is null.

Optional named parameters

When calling a function, you can specify named parameters using *paramName: value*. For example:

```dart
enableFlags(bold: true, hidden: false);
```

When defining a function, use {*param1, param2, ...*} to specify named parameters:

```
/// Sets the [bold] and [hidden] flags to the values you specify.
enableFlags({bool bold, bool hidden}) {
  // ...
}
```

Use a colon (:) to specify default values:

```
/**
 * Sets the [bold] and [hidden] flags to the values you specify,
 * defaulting to false.
 */
enableFlags({bool bold: false, bool hidden: false}) {
  // ...
}

enableFlags(bold: true); // bold will be true; hidden will be false.
```

Optional positional parameters

Wrapping a set of function parameters in [] marks them as optional positional parameters:

```
String say(String from, String msg, [String device]) {
  var result = '$from says $msg';
  if (device != null) {
    result = '$result with a $device';
  }
  return result;
}
```

Here's an example of calling this function without the optional parameter:

```
assert(say('Bob', 'Howdy') == 'Bob says Howdy');
```

And here's an example of calling this function with the third parameter:

```
assert(say('Bob', 'Howdy', 'smoke signal') ==
  'Bob says Howdy with a smoke signal');
```

Use = to specify default values:

```
String say(String from, String msg,
  [String device='carrier pigeon', String mood]) {
  var result = '$from says $msg';
  if (device != null) {
    result = '$result with a $device';
  }
  if (mood != null) {
    result = '$result (in a $mood mood)';
  }
  return result;
}
```

```
assert(say('Bob', 'Howdy') == 'Bob says Howdy with a carrier pigeon');
```

The main() Function

Every app must have a top-level `main()` function, which serves as the entrypoint to the app. The `main()` function returns void and has an optional `List<String>` parameter for arguments.

Here's an example of the `main()` function for a web app:

```
main() {
  querySelector("#sample_text_id")
    ..text = "Click me!"
    ..onClick.listen(reverseText);
}
```

 The .. operator in the preceding code is a cascade operator, which allows you to perform multiple operations on the members of a single object. You'll find out more in "Classes" on page 38.

Here's an example of the `main()` function for a command-line app that takes arguments:

```
// Run the app like this: dart args.dart 1 test
void main(List<String> arguments) {
  print(arguments);

  assert(arguments.length == 2);
  assert(int.parse(arguments[0]) == 1);
  assert(arguments[1] == 'test');
}
```

You can use the args library[13] to define and parse command-line arguments.

Functions as First-Class Objects

You can pass a function as a parameter to another function. For example:

```
printElement(element) {
  print(element);
}

var list = [1,2,3];
list.forEach(printElement); // Pass printElement as a parameter.
```

You can also assign a function to a variable, such as:

13. *http://api.dartlang.org/args.html*

```
var loudify = (msg) => '!!! ${msg.toUpperCase()} !!!';
assert(loudify('hello') == '!!! HELLO !!!');
```

Lexical Scope

Dart is a lexically scoped language, which means that the scope of variables is determined statically, simply by the layout of the code. You can "follow the curly braces outwards" to see if a variable is in scope.

Here is an example of nested functions with variables at each scope level:

```
var topLevel = true;
main() {
    var insideMain = true;

    myFunction() {
      var insideFunction = true;

      nestedFunction() {
        var insideNestedFunction = true;
        assert(topLevel);
        assert(insideMain);
        assert(insideFunction);
        assert(insideNestedFunction);
      }
    }
}
```

Notice how nestedFunction() can use variables from every level, all the way up to the top level.

Lexical Closures

A *closure* is a function object that has access to variables in its lexical scope, even when the function is used outside of its original scope.

Functions can close over variables defined in surrounding scopes. In the following example, adder() captures the variable addBy. Wherever the returned function goes, it remembers addBy:

```
/// Returns a function that adds [addBy] to a number.
Function makeAdder(num addBy) {
  adder(num i) {
    return addBy + i;
  }
  return adder;
}

main() {
  var add2 = makeAdder(2); // Create a function that adds 2.
  var add4 = makeAdder(4); // Create a function that adds 4.
```

```
    assert(add2(3) == 5);
    assert(add4(3) == 7);
}
```

Testing Functions for Equality

Here's an example of testing top-level functions, static methods, and instance methods
for equality:

```
foo() {}                // A top-level function

class SomeClass {
  static void bar() {} // A static method
  void baz() {}        // An instance method
}

main() {
  var x;

  // Comparing top-level functions.
  x = foo;
  assert(x == foo);

  // Comparing static methods.
  x = SomeClass.bar;
  assert(x == SomeClass.bar);

  // Comparing instance methods.
  var v = new SomeClass();
  var w = new SomeClass();
  var y = v;
  x = v.baz;

  assert(x == y.baz);
  assert(v.baz != w.baz);
}
```

Return Values

All functions return a value. If no return value is specified, the statement `return`
`null;` is implicitly appended to the function body.

Operators

Dart defines the operators shown in Table 2-2. You can override many of these operators,
as described in "Overridable operators" on page 46.

Table 2-2. Operators and their precedence

Description	Operator
unary postfix	*expr*++ *expr*-- () [] .
unary prefix	-*expr* !*expr* ~*expr* ++*expr* --*expr*
multiplicative	* / % ~/
additive	+ -
shift	<< >>
bitwise AND	&
bitwise XOR	^
bitwise OR	|
relational and type test	>= > <= < as is is!
equality	== !=
logical AND	&&
logical OR	||
conditional	*expr1* ? *expr2* : *expr3*
cascade	..
assignment	= *= /= ~/= %= += -= <<= >>= &= ^= |=

When you use operators, you create *expressions*. Here are some examples of operator expressions:

```
a++
a + b
a = b
a == b
a? b: c
a is T
```

In Table 2-2, each operator has higher precedence than the operators in the rows below it. For example, the multiplicative operator % has higher precedence than (and thus executes before) the equality operator ==, which has higher precedence than the logical AND operator &&. That precedence means that the following two lines of code execute the same way:

```
if ((n % i == 0) && (d % i == 0)) // Parens improve readability.
if (n % i == 0 && d % i == 0)     // Harder to read, but equivalent.
```

 For operators that work on two operands, the leftmost operand determines which version of the operator is used. For example, if you have a Vector object and a Point object, aVector + aPoint uses the Vector version of +.

Arithmetic Operators

Dart supports the usual arithmetic operators, as shown in Table 2-3.

Table 2-3. Arithmetic operators

Operator	Meaning
+	Add
−	Subtract
-expr	Unary minus, also known as negation (reverse the sign of the expression)
*	Multiply
/	Divide
~/	Divide, returning an integer result
%	Get the remainder of an integer division (modulo)

For example:

```
assert(2 + 3 == 5);
assert(2 - 3 == -1);
assert(2 * 3 == 6);
assert(5 / 2 == 2.5);    // Result is a double
assert(5 ~/ 2 == 2);     // Result is an integer
assert(5 % 2 == 1);      // Remainder

print('5/2 = ${5~/2} remainder ${5%2}'); // 5/2 = 2 remainder 1
```

Dart also supports both prefix and postfix increment and decrement operators.

Table 2-4. Increment and decrement operators

Operator	Meaning
++var	var = var + 1 (expression value is var + 1)
var++	var = var + 1 (expression value is var)
--var	var = var − 1 (expression value is var − 1)
var--	var = var − 1 (expression value is var)

For example:

```
var a, b;

a = 0;
b = ++a;          // Increment a before b gets its value.
assert(a == b);   // 1 == 1

a = 0;
b = a++;          // Increment a AFTER b gets its value.
assert(a != b);   // 1 != 0
```

```
a = 0;
b = --a;           // Decrement a before b gets its value.
assert(a == b);    // -1 == -1

a = 0;
b = a--;           // Decrement a AFTER b gets its value.
assert(a != b) ;   // -1 != 0
```

Equality and Relational Operators

Table 2-5 lists the meanings of equality and relational operators.

Table 2-5. Equality and relational operators

Operator	Meaning
==	Equal; see the following discussion
!=	Not equal
>	Greater than
<	Less than
>=	Greater than or equal to
<=	Less than or equal to

To test whether two objects *x* and *y* represent the same thing, use the == operator. (In the rare case where you need to know whether two objects are the exact same object, use the identical()[14] function instead.) Here's how the == operator works:

1. If *x* or *y* is null, return true if both are null, and false if only one is null.

2. Return the result of the method invocation *x*.==(*y*). (That's right, operators such as == are methods that are invoked on their first operand. You can even override many operators, including ==, as you'll see in "Overridable operators" on page 46.)

Here's an example of using each of the equality and relational operators:

```
assert(2 == 2);
assert(2 != 3);
assert(3 > 2);
assert(2 < 3);
assert(3 >= 3);
assert(2 <= 3);
```

Type Test Operators

The as, is, and is! operators are handy for checking types at runtime (see Table 2-6).

---

14. *http://api.dartlang.org/dart_core.html#identical*

Table 2-6. Type test operators

Operator	Meaning
as	Typecast
is	True if the object has the specified type
is!	False if the object has the specified type

The result of obj is T is true if obj implements the interface specified by T. For example, obj is Object is always true.

Use the as operator to cast an object to a particular type. In general, you should use it as a shorthand for an is test on an object followed by an expression using that object. For example, consider the following code:

```
if (person is Person) {              // Type check
  person.firstName = 'Bob';
}
```

You can make the code shorter using the as operator:

```
(person as Person).firstName = 'Bob';
```

 The code isn't equivalent. If person is null or not a Person, the first example (with is) does nothing; the second (with as) throws an exception.

Assignment Operators

As you've already seen, you assign values using the = operator. You can also use compound assignment operators such as +=, which combine an operation with an assignment (see Table 2-7).

Table 2-7. Assignment operators

```
=    -=  /=   %=   >>=  ^=
+=  *=  ~/=  <<=  &=   |=
```

Here's how compound assignment operators work:

	Compound assignment	Equivalent expression
For an operator *op*:	a *op*= b	a = a *op* b
Example:	a += b	a = a + b

The following example uses both assignment and compound assignment operators:

```
var a = 2;              // Assign using =
a *= 3;                 // Assign and multiply: a = a * 3
assert(a == 6);
```

Logical Operators

You can invert or combine boolean expressions using the logical operators (see Table 2-8).

Table 2-8. Logical operators

Operator	Meaning
!*expr*	inverts the following expression (changes false to true, and vice versa)
||	logical OR
&&	logical AND

Here's an example of using the logical operators:

```
if (!done && (col == 0 || col == 3)) {
  // ...Do something...
}
```

Bitwise and Shift Operators

You can manipulate the individual bits of numbers in Dart. Usually, you'd use these bitwise and shift operators with integers, as shown in Table 2-9.

Table 2-9. Bitwise and shift operators

Operator	Meaning
&	AND
|	OR
^	XOR
~*expr*	Unary bitwise complement (0s become 1s; 1s become 0s)
<<	Shift left
>>	Shift right

Here's an example of using bitwise and shift operators:

```
final value = 0x22;
final bitmask = 0x0f;

assert((value & bitmask)  == 0x02); // AND
assert((value & ~bitmask) == 0x20); // AND NOT
assert((value | bitmask)  == 0x2f); // OR
assert((value ^ bitmask)  == 0x2d); // XOR
assert((value << 4)       == 0x220); // Shift left
assert((value >> 4)       == 0x02); // Shift right
```

Other Operators

A few operators remain (see Table 2-10), most of which you've already seen in other examples.

Table 2-10. Other operators

Operator	Name	Meaning
()	Function application	Represents a function call
[]	List access	Refers to the value at the specified index in the list
expr1? *expr2*: *expr3*	Conditional	If *expr1* is true, executes *expr2*; otherwise, executes *expr3*
.	Member access	Refers to a property of an expression; example: foo.bar selects property bar from expression foo
..	Cascade	Allows you to perform multiple operations on the members of a single object; described in "Classes" on page 38

Control Flow Statements

You can control the flow of your Dart code using any of the following:

- if and else
- for loops
- while and do-while loops
- break and continue
- switch and case
- assert

You can also affect the control flow using try-catch and throw, as explained in "Exceptions" on page 36.

If and Else

Dart supports if statements with optional else statements, as the next sample shows. Also see conditional expressions (?:), which are covered in "Other Operators":

```
if (isRaining()) {
  you.bringRainCoat();
} else if (isSnowing()) {
  you.wearJacket();
} else {
  car.putTopDown();
}
```

Remember, unlike JavaScript, Dart treats all values other than `true` as `false`. See "Booleans" on page 18 for more information.

For Loops

You can iterate with the standard `for` loop. For example:

```
var message = new StringBuffer("Dart is fun");
for (var i = 0; i < 5; i++) {
  message.write('!');
}
```

Closures inside of Dart's `for` loops capture the value of the index, avoiding a common pitfall found in JavaScript. For example, consider:

```
var callbacks = [];
for (var i = 0; i < 2; i++) {
  callbacks.add(() => print(i));
}
callbacks.forEach((c) => c());
```

The output is 0 and then 1, as expected. In contrast, the example would print 2 and then 2 in JavaScript.

If the object that you are iterating over is an Iterable, you can use the `forEach()`[15] method. Using `forEach()` is a good option if you don't need to know the current iteration counter:

```
candidates.forEach((candidate) => candidate.interview());
```

Iterable classes such as List and Set also support the `for-in` form of iteration, which is described in "Iteration" on page 75:

```
var collection = [0, 1, 2];
for (var x in collection) {
  print(x);
}
```

While and Do-While

A `while` loop evaluates the condition before the loop:

```
while(!isDone()) {
  doSomething();
}
```

A do-while loop evaluates the condition *after* the loop:

---

15. *http://api.dartlang.org/dart_core/Iterable.html#forEach*

```
do {
  printLine();
} while (!atEndOfPage());
```

Break and Continue

Use break to stop looping:

```
while (true) {
  if (shutDownRequested()) break;
  processIncomingRequests();
}
```

Use continue to skip to the next loop iteration:

```
for (int i = 0; i < candidates.length; i++) {
  var candidate = candidates[i];
  if (candidate.yearsExperience < 5) {
    continue;
  }
  candidate.interview();
}
```

You might write that example differently if you're using an Iterable[16] such as a list or set:

```
candidates.where((c) => c.yearsExperience >= 5)
          .forEach((c) => c.interview());
```

Switch and Case

Switch statements in Dart compare integer, string, or compile-time constants using ==. The compared objects must all be instances of the same class (and not of any of its subtypes), and the class must not override ==.

Each non-empty case clause ends with a break statement, as a rule. Other valid ways to end a non-empty case clause are a continue, throw, or return statement.

Use a default clause to execute code when no case clause matches:

---

16. *http://api.dartlang.org/dart_core/Iterable.html*

```
var command = 'OPEN';
switch (command) {
  case 'CLOSED':
    executeClosed();
    break;
  case 'PENDING':
    executePending();
    break;
  case 'APPROVED':
    executeApproved();
    break;
  case 'DENIED':
    executeDenied();
    break;
  case 'OPEN':
    executeOpen();
    break;
  default:
    executeUnknown();
}
```

The following example omits the break statement in the case clause, thus generating an error:

```
var command = 'OPEN';
switch (command) {
  case 'OPEN':
    executeOpen();
    // ERROR: Missing break causes an exception to be thrown!!

  case 'CLOSED':
    executeClosed();
    break;
}
```

However, Dart does support empty case clauses, allowing a form of fall-through:

```
var command = 'CLOSED';
switch (command) {
  case 'CLOSED':      // Empty case falls through.
  case 'NOW_CLOSED':
    // Runs for both CLOSED and NOW_CLOSED.
    executeNowClosed();
    break;
}
```

If you really want fall-through, you can use a continue statement and a label:

```
var command = 'CLOSED';
switch (command) {
  case 'CLOSED':
    executeClosed();
    continue nowClosed; // Continues executing at the nowClosed label.
```

```
nowClosed:
  case 'NOW_CLOSED':
    // Runs for both CLOSED and NOW_CLOSED.
    executeNowClosed();
    break;
}
```

A `case` clause can have local variables, which are visible only inside the scope of that clause.

Assert

Use an `assert` statement to disrupt normal execution if a boolean condition is false. You can find examples of assert statements throughout this tour. Here are some more:

```
assert(text != null);  // Make sure the variable has a non-null value.
assert(number < 100);  // Make sure the value is less than 100.
assert(urlString.startsWith('https')); // Make sure this is an HTTPS URL.
```

 Assert statements work only in checked mode. They have no effect in production mode.

Inside the parentheses after `assert`, you can put any expression that resolves to a boolean value or to a function. If the expression's value or function's return value is true, the assertion succeeds and execution continues. If it's false, the assertion fails and an exception (an AssertionError[17]) is thrown.

Exceptions

Your Dart code can throw and catch exceptions. Exceptions are errors indicating that something unexpected happened. If the exception isn't caught, the isolate that raised the exception is suspended, and typically the isolate and its program are terminated.

In contrast to Java, all of Dart's exceptions are unchecked exceptions. Methods do not declare which exceptions they might throw, and you are not required to catch any exceptions.

17. *http://api.dartlang.org/dart_core/AssertionError.html*

Dart provides Exception[18] and Error[19] types, as well as numerous predefined subtypes. You can, of course, define your own exceptions. However, Dart programs can throw any non-null object—not just Exception and Error objects—as an exception.

Throw

Here's an example of throwing, or *raising*, an exception:

```
throw new ExpectException('Value must be greater than zero');
```

You can also throw arbitrary objects:

```
throw 'Out of llamas!';
```

Because throwing an exception is an expression, you can throw exceptions in => statements, as well as anywhere else that allows expressions:

```
distanceTo(Point other) => throw new UnimplementedError();
```

Catch

Catching, or capturing, an exception stops the exception from propagating. Catching an exception gives you a chance to handle it:

```
try {
  breedMoreLlamas();
} on OutOfLlamasException {
  buyMoreLlamas();
}
```

To handle code that can throw more than one type of exception, you can specify multiple catch clauses. The first catch clause that matches the thrown object's type handles the exception. If the catch clause does not specify a type, that clause can handle any type of thrown object:

```
try {
  breedMoreLlamas();
} on OutOfLlamasException {          // A specific exception
  buyMoreLlamas();
} on Exception catch(e) {            // Anything else that is an exception
  print('Unknown exception: $e');
} catch(e) {                        // No specified type, handles all
  print('Something really unknown: $e');
}
```

18. *http://api.dartlang.org/dart_core/Exception.html*

19. *http://api.dartlang.org/docs/continuous/dart_core/Error.html*

As the preceding code shows, you can use either on or catch or both. Use on when you need to specify the exception type. Use catch when your exception handler needs the exception object.

Finally

To ensure that some code runs whether or not an exception is thrown, use a finally clause. If no catch clause matches the exception, the exception is propagated after the finally clause runs:

```
try {
  breedMoreLlamas();
} finally {
  cleanLlamaStalls();  // Always clean up, even if an exception is thrown.
}
```

The finally clause runs after any matching catch clauses:

```
try {
  breedMoreLlamas();
} catch(e) {
  print('Error: $e');  // Handle the exception first.
} finally {
  cleanLlamaStalls();  // Then clean up.
}
```

Learn more by reading "Exceptions" on page 75.

Classes

Dart is an object-oriented language with classes and mixin-based inheritance. Every object is an instance of a class, and all classes descend from Object.[20] *Mixin-based inheritance* means that although every class (except for Object) has exactly one superclass, a class body can be reused in multiple class hierarchies.

To create an object, you can use the new keyword with a *constructor* for a class. Constructor names can be either *ClassName* or *ClassName.identifier*. For example:

```
var jsonData = JSON.decode('{"x":1, "y":2}');

var p1 = new Point(2,2);                 // Create a Point using Point().
var p2 = new Point.fromJson(jsonData); // Create a Point using Point.fromJson().
```

Objects have *members* consisting of functions and data (*methods* and *instance variables*, respectively). When you call a method, you *invoke* it on an object: the method has access to that object's functions and data.

---

20. *http://api.dartlang.org/dart_core/Object.html*

Use a dot (.) to refer to an instance variable or method:

```
var p = new Point(2,2);

p.y = 3;              // Set the value of the instance variable y.
assert(p.y == 3);     // Get the value of y.

num distance = p.distanceTo(new Point(4,4)); // Invoke distanceTo() on p.
```

Use the cascade operator (..) when you want to perform a series of operations on the members of a single object:

```
querySelector('#button')
    ..text = 'Click to Confirm'                 // Get an object. Use its
    ..classes.add('important')                  // instance variables
    ..onClick.listen((e) => window.alert('Confirmed!')); // and methods.
```

Some classes provide constant constructors. To create a compile-time constant using a constant constructor, use const instead of new:

```
var p = const ImmutablePoint(2,2);
```

Constructing two identical compile-time constants results in a single, canonical instance:

```
var a = const ImmutablePoint(1, 1);
var b = const ImmutablePoint(1, 1);

assert(identical(a,b)); // They are the same instance!
```

The following sections discuss how to implement classes.

Instance Variables

Here's how you declare instance variables:

```
class Point {
  num x;        // Declare an instance variable (x), initially null.
  num y;        // Declare y, initially null.
  num z = 0;    // Declare z, initially 0.
}
```

All uninitialized instance variables have the value null.

All instance variables generate an implicit *getter* method. Non-final instance variables also generate an implicit *setter* method. For details, see "Getters and setters" on page 44:

```
class Point {
  num x;
  num y;
}

main() {
  var point = new Point();
```

```
    point.x = 4;           // Use the setter method for x.
    assert(point.x == 4);  // Use the getter method for x.
    assert(point.y == null); // Values default to null.
  }
```

If you initialize an instance variable where it is declared (instead of in a constructor or method), the value is set when the instance is created, which is before the constructor and its initializer list execute.

Constructors

Declare a constructor by creating a function with the same name as its class (plus, optionally, an additional identifier as described in "Named constructors" on page 41). The most common form of constructor, the generative constructor, creates a new instance of a class:

```
class Point {
  num x;
  num y;

  Point(num x, num y) {
    // There's a better way to do this, stay tuned.
    this.x = x;
    this.y = y;
  }
}
```

The this keyword refers to the current instance.

 Use this only when there is a name conflict. Otherwise, Dart style omits the this.

The pattern of assigning a constructor argument to an instance variable is so common, Dart has syntactic sugar to make it easy:

```
class Point {
  num x;
  num y;

  // Syntactic sugar for setting x and y before the constructor body runs.
  Point(this.x, this.y);
}
```

Default constructors

If you don't declare a constructor, a default constructor is provided for you. The default constructor has no arguments and invokes the no-argument constructor in the superclass.

Constructors aren't inherited

Subclasses don't inherit constructors from their superclass. A subclass that declares no constructors has only the default (no argument, no name) constructor.

Named constructors

Use a named constructor to implement multiple constructors for a class or to provide extra clarity:

```
class Point {
  num x;
  num y;

  Point(this.x, this.y);

  // Named constructor
  Point.fromJson(Map json) {
    x = json['x'];
    y = json['y'];
  }
}
```

Remember that constructors are not inherited, which means that a superclass's named constructor is not inherited by a subclass. If you want a subclass to be created with a named constructor defined in the superclass, you must implement that constructor in the subclass.

Invoking a non-default superclass constructor

By default, a constructor in a subclass calls the superclass's unnamed, no-argument constructor. If the superclass doesn't have such a constructor, then you must manually call one of the constructors in the superclass. Specify the superclass constructor after a colon (:), just before the constructor body (if any):

```
class Person {
  Person.fromJson(Map data) {
    print('in Person');
  }
}

class Employee extends Person {
  // Person does not have a default constructor;
  // you must call super.fromJson(data).
```

```
    Employee.fromJson(Map data) : super.fromJson(data) {
      print('in Employee');
    }
  }

  main() {
    var emp = new Employee.fromJson({});

    // Prints:
    // in Person
    // in Employee
  }
```

Because the arguments to the superclass constructor are evaluated before invoking the constructor, an argument can be an expression such as a function call:

```
  class Employee extends Person {
    ...
    Employee() : super.fromJson(findDefaultData());
  }
```

Arguments to the superclass constructor do not have access to this. For example, arguments can call static methods but not instance methods.

Initializer list

Besides invoking a superclass constructor, you can also initialize instance variables before the constructor body runs. Separate initializers with commas:

```
  class Point {
    num x;
    num y;

    Point(this.x, this.y);

    // Initializer list sets instance variables before the constructor body runs.
    Point.fromJson(Map json) : x = json['x'], y = json['y'] {
      print('In Point.fromJson(): ($x, $y)');
    }
  }
```

The righthand side of an initializer does not have access to this.

Redirecting constructors

Sometimes a constructor's only purpose is to redirect to another constructor in the same class. A redirecting constructor's body is empty, with the constructor call appearing after a colon (:):

```
class Point {
  num x;
  num y;

  Point(this.x, this.y);                    // The main constructor for this class.
  Point.alongXAxis(num x) : this(x, 0); // Delegates to the main constructor.
}
```

Constant constructors

If your class produces objects that never change, you can make these objects compile-time constants. To do this, define a const constructor and make sure that all instance variables are final.

```
class ImmutablePoint {
  final num x;
  final num y;
  const ImmutablePoint(this.x, this.y);
  static final ImmutablePoint origin = const ImmutablePoint(0, 0);
}
```

Factory constructors

Use the factory keyword when implementing a constructor that doesn't always create a new instance of its class. For example, a factory constructor might return an instance from a cache, or it might return an instance of a subtype.

The following example demonstrates a factory constructor returning objects from a cache:

```
class Logger {
  final String name;
  bool mute = false;

  // _cache is library-private, thanks to the _ in front of its name.
  static final Map<String, Logger> _cache = <String, Logger>{};

  factory Logger(String name) {
    if (_cache.containsKey(name)) {
      return _cache[name];
    } else {
      final logger = new Logger._internal(name);
      _cache[name] = logger;
      return logger;
    }
```

```
  }

  Logger._internal(this.name);

  void log(String msg) {
    if (!mute) {
      print(msg);
    }
  }
}
```

 Factory constructors have no access to this.

To invoke a factory constructor, you use the new keyword:

```
var logger = new Logger('UI');
logger.log('Button clicked');
```

Methods

Methods are functions that provide behavior for an object.

Instance methods

Instance methods on objects can access instance variables and this. The distance
To() method in the following sample is an example of an instance method:

```
import 'dart:math';

class Point {
  num x;
  num y;
  Point(this.x, this.y);

  num distanceTo(Point other) {
    var dx = x - other.x;
    var dy = y - other.y;
    return sqrt(dx * dx + dy * dy);
  }
}
```

Getters and setters

Getters and setters are special methods that provide read and write access to an object's
properties. Recall that each instance variable has an implicit getter, plus a setter if ap-

propriate. You can create additional properties by implementing getters and setters, using the `get` and `set` keywords:

```
class Rectangle {
  num left;
  num top;
  num width;
  num height;

  Rectangle(this.left, this.top, this.width, this.height);

  // Define two calculated properties: right and bottom.
  num get right             => left + width;
      set right(num value)  => left = value - width;
  num get bottom            => top + height;
      set bottom(num value) => top = value - height;
}

main() {
  var rect = new Rectangle(3, 4, 20, 15);
  assert(rect.left == 3);
  rect.right = 12;
  assert(rect.left == -8);
}
```

With getters and setters, you can start with instance variables, later wrapping them with methods, all without changing client code.

 Operators such as increment (++) work in the expected way, whether or not a getter is explicitly defined. To avoid any unexpected side effects, the operator calls the getter exactly once, saving its value in a temporary variable.

Abstract methods

Instance, getter, and setter methods can be abstract, defining an interface but leaving its implementation up to other classes. To make a method abstract, use a semicolon (;) instead of a method body:

```
abstract class Doer {
  // ...Define instance variables and methods...

  void doSomething(); // Define an abstract method.
}

class EffectiveDoer extends Doer {
  void doSomething() {
    // ...Provide an implementation, so the method is not abstract here...
```

```
    }
  }
```

Calling an abstract method results in a runtime error. Also see "Abstract Classes" on page 47.

Overridable operators

You can override the operators shown in Table 2-11. For example, if you define a Vector class, you might define a + method to add two vectors.

Table 2-11. Operators that can be overridden

<	+	|	[]
>	/	^	[]=
<=	~/	&	~
>=	*	<<	==
-	%	>>	

Here's an example of a class that overrides the + and - operators:

```
class Vector {
  final int x;
  final int y;
  const Vector(this.x, this.y);

  Vector operator +(Vector v) { // Overrides + (a + b).
    return new Vector(x + v.x, y + v.y);
  }

  Vector operator -(Vector v) { // Overrides - (a - b).
    return new Vector(x - v.x, y - v.y);
  }
}

main() {
  final v = new Vector(2,3);
  final w = new Vector(2,2);

  assert(v.x == 2 && v.y == 3);           // v   == (2,3)
  assert((v+w).x == 4 && (v+w).y == 5); // v+w == (4,5)
  assert((v-w).x == 0 && (v-w).y == 1); // v-w == (0,1)
}
```

If you override ==, you should also override Object's hashCode getter. For an example of overriding == and hashCode, see "Implementing map keys" on page 74.

For more information on overriding, in general, see "Extending a Class" on page 48.

Abstract Classes

Use the `abstract` modifier to define an *abstract class*—a class that can't be instantiated. Abstract classes are useful for defining interfaces, often with some implementation. If you want your abstract class to appear to be instantiable, define a factory constructor (page 43).

Abstract classes often have abstract methods (page 45). Here's an example of declaring an abstract class that has an abstract method:

```
// This class is declared abstract and thus can't be instantiated.
abstract class AbstractContainer {
  // ...Define constructors, fields, methods...

  void updateChildren(); // Abstract method.
}
```

The following class isn't abstract, and thus can be instantiated even though it defines an abstract method:

```
class SpecializedContainer extends AbstractContainer {
  // ...Define more constructors, fields, methods...

  void updateChildren() {
    // ...Implement updateChildren()...
  }
// Abstract method causes a warning but doesn't prevent instantiation.
  void doSomething();
}
```

Implicit Interfaces

Every class implicitly defines an interface containing all the instance members of the class and of any interfaces it implements. If you want to create a class A that supports class B's API without inheriting B's implementation, class A should implement the B interface.

A class implements one or more interfaces by declaring them in an `implements` clause and then providing the APIs required by the interfaces. For example:

```
// A person. The implicit interface contains greet().
class Person {
  final _name;          // In the interface, but visible only in this library,
  Person(this._name);   // Not in the interface, since this is a constructor.
  String greet(who) => 'Hello, $who. I am $_name.'; // In the interface.
}

// An implementation of the Person interface.
class Imposter implements Person {
  final _name = "";     // We have to define this, but we don't use it.
  String greet(who) => 'Hi $who. Do you know who I am?';
```

```
  }

  greetBob(Person person) => person.greet('bob');

  main() {
    print(greetBob(new Person('kathy')));
    print(greetBob(new Imposter()));
  }
```

Here's an example of specifying that a class implements multiple interfaces:

```
class Point implements Comparable, Location {
  // ...
}
```

Extending a Class

Use extends to create a subclass, and super to refer to the superclass:

```
class Television {
  void turnOn() {
    _illuminateDisplay();
    _activateIrSensor();
  }
  ...
}

class SmartTelevision extends Television {
  void turnOn() {
    super.turnOn();
    _bootNetworkInterface();
    _initializeMemory();
    _upgradeApps();
  }
  ...
}
```

Subclasses can override instance methods, getters, and setters. Here's an example of overriding the Object class's noSuchMethod() method, which is called whenever code attempts to use a non-existent method or instance variable:

```
class A {
  // Unless you override noSuchMethod, using a non-existent member
  // results in a NoSuchMethodError.
  void noSuchMethod(Invocation mirror) {
    print('You tried to use a non-existent member: ${mirror.memberName}');
  }
}
```

You can use the @override annotation to indicate that you are intentionally overriding a member:

```
class A {
  @override
  void noSuchMethod(Invocation mirror) {
    // ...
  }
}
```

If you use noSuchMethod() to implement every possible getter, setter, and method for a class, then you can use the @proxy annotation to avoid warnings:

```
@proxy
class A {
  void noSuchMethod(Invocation mirror) {
    // ...
  }
}
```

For more information on annotations, see "Metadata" on page 57.

Adding Features to a Class: Mixins

Mixins are a way of reusing a class's code in multiple class hierarchies.

To use a mixin, use the with keyword followed by one or more mixin names. The following example shows two classes that use mixins:

```
class Musician extends Performer with Musical {
  ...
}

class Maestro extends Person with Musical, Aggressive, Demented {
  Maestro(String maestroName) {
    name = maestroName;
    canConduct = true;
  }
}
```

To implement a mixin, create a class that extends Object, declares no constructors, and has no calls to super. For example:

```
abstract class Musical {
  bool canPlayPiano = false;
  bool canCompose = false;
  bool canConduct = false;

  void entertainMe() {
    if (canPlayPiano) {
      print('Playing piano');
    } else if (canConduct) {
      print('Waving hands');
    } else {
      print('Humming to self');
```

```
    }
  }
}
```

For more information, see the article "Mixins in Dart[21]."

Class Variables and Methods

Use the `static` keyword to implement class-wide variables and methods.

Static variables

Static variables (class variables) are useful for class-wide state and constants:

```
class Color {
  static const RED = const Color('red'); // A constant static variable.
  final String name;                     // An instance variable.
  const Color(this.name);                // A constant constructor.
}

main() {
  assert(Color.RED.name == 'red');
}
```

Static variables aren't initialized until they're used.

Static methods

Static methods (class methods) do not operate on an instance, and thus do not have access to `this`. For example:

```
import 'dart:math';

class Point {
  num x;
  num y;
  Point(this.x, this.y);

  static num distanceBetween(Point a, Point b) {
    var dx = a.x - b.x;
    var dy = a.y - b.y;
    return sqrt(dx * dx + dy * dy);
  }
}

main() {
  var a = new Point(2, 2);
  var b = new Point(4, 4);
  var distance = Point.distanceBetween(a,b);
```

21. *http://www.dartlang.org/articles/mixins/*

```
    assert(distance < 2.9 && distance > 2.8);
}
```

 Consider using top-level functions, instead of static methods, for common or widely used utilities and functionality.

You can use static methods as compile-time constants. For example, you can pass a static method as a parameter to a constant constructor.

Generics

If you look at the API documentation for the basic array type, List[22], you'll see that the type is actually List<E>. The <...> notation marks List as a *generic* (or *parameterized*) type—a type that has formal type parameters. By convention, type variables have single-letter names, such as E, T, S, K, and V.

Why Use Generics?

Because types are optional in Dart, you never *have* to use generics. You might *want* to, though, for the same reason you might want to use other types in your code: types (generic or not) let you document and annotate your code, making your intent clearer.

For example, if you intend for a list to contain only strings, you can declare it as List<String> (read that as "list of string"). That way you, your fellow programmers, and your tools (such as Dart Editor and the Dart VM in checked mode) can detect that assigning a non-string to the list is probably a mistake. Here's an example:

```
var names = new List<String>();
names.addAll(['Seth', 'Kathy', 'Lars']);
// ...
names.add(42); // Fails in checked mode (succeeds in production mode).
```

Another reason for using generics is to reduce code duplication. Generics let you share a single interface and implementation between many types, while still taking advantage of checked mode and static analysis early warnings. For example, say you create an interface for caching an object:

```
abstract class ObjectCache {
  Object getByKey(String key);
  setByKey(String key, Object value);
}
```

22. *http://api.dartlang.org/dart_core/List.html*

You discover that you want a string-specific version of this interface, so you create another interface:

```
abstract class StringCache {
  String getByKey(String key);
  setByKey(String key, String value);
}
```

Later, you decide you want a number-specific version of this interface...you get the idea.

Generic types can save you the trouble of creating all these interfaces. Instead, you can create a single interface that takes a type parameter:

```
abstract class Cache<T> {
  T getByKey(String key);
  setByKey(String key, T value);
}
```

In this code, T is the stand-in type. It's a placeholder that you can think of as a type that a developer will define later.

Using Collection Literals

List and map literals can be parameterized. Parameterized literals are just like the literals you've already seen, except that you add *<type>* (for lists) or *<keyType, valueType>* (for maps) before the opening bracket. You might use parameterized literals when you want type warnings in checked mode. Here is an example of using typed literals:

```
var names = <String>['Seth', 'Kathy', 'Lars'];
var pages = <String, String>{
    'index.html':'Homepage',
    'robots.txt':'Hints for web robots',
    'humans.txt':'We are people, not machines' };
```

Using Parameterized Types with Constructors

To specify one or more types when using a constructor, put the types in angle brackets (`<...>`) just after the class name. For example:

```
var names = new List<String>();
names.addAll(['Seth', 'Kathy', 'Lars']);
var nameSet = new Set<String>.from(names);
```

The following code creates a map that has integer keys and values of type View:

```
var views = new Map<int, View>();
```

Generic Collections and the Types They Contain

Dart generic types are *reified*, which means that they carry their type information around at runtime. For example, you can test the type of a collection, even in production mode:

```
var names = new List<String>();
names.addAll(['Seth', 'Kathy', 'Lars']);
print(names is List<String>); // true
```

However, the is expression checks the type of the *collection* only—not of the objects inside it. In production mode, a List<String> might have some non-string items in it. The solution is to either check each item's type or wrap item-manipulation code in an exception handler (see "Exceptions" on page 36).

> In contrast, generics in Java use *erasure*, which means that generic type parameters are removed at runtime. In Java, you can test whether an object is a List, but you can't test whether it's a List<String>.

For more information about generics, see "Optional Types in Dart[23]."

Libraries and Visibility

The import, part, and library directives can help you create a modular and shareable code base. Libraries not only provide APIs, but are a unit of privacy: identifiers that start with an underscore (_) are visible only inside the library. *Every Dart app is a library*, even if it doesn't use a library directive.

Libraries can be distributed using packages. See "pub: The Dart Package Manager" on page 104 for information about pub, a package manager included in the SDK.

Using Libraries

Use import to specify how a namespace from one library is used in the scope of another library.

For example, Dart web apps generally use the dart:html[24] library, which they can import like this:

```
import 'dart:html';
```

The only required argument to import is a URI[25] specifying the library. For built-in libraries, the URI has the special dart: scheme. For other libraries, you can use a file system path or the package: scheme. The package: scheme specifies libraries provided by a package manager such as the pub tool. For example:

---

23. *http://www.dartlang.org/articles/optional-types/*
24. *http://api.dartlang.org/html.html*
25. URI stands for *uniform resource identifier*. URLs (*uniform resource locators*) are a common kind of URI.

```
import 'dart:io';
import 'package:mylib/mylib.dart';
import 'package:utils/utils.dart';
```

Specifying a library prefix

If you import two libraries that have conflicting identifiers, then you can specify a prefix for one or both libraries. For example, if library1 and library2 both have an Element class, then you might have code like this:

```
import 'package:lib1/lib1.dart';
import 'package:lib2/lib2.dart' as lib2;
// ...
var element1 = new Element();      // Uses Element from lib1.
var element2 = new lib2.Element(); // Uses Element from lib2.
```

Importing only part of a library

If you want to use only part of a library, you can selectively import the library. For example:

```
import 'package:lib1/lib1.dart' show foo; // Import only foo.
import 'package:lib2/lib2.dart' hide foo; // Import all names EXCEPT foo.
```

Implementing Libraries

Use library to name a library, and part to specify additional files in the library.

 You don't have to use library in an app (a file that has a top-level main() function), but doing so lets you implement the app in multiple files.

Declaring a library

Use library *identifier* to specify the name of the current library:

```
library ballgame;   // Declare that this is a library named ballgame.

import 'dart:html'; // This app uses the HTML library.
// ...Code goes here...
```

Associating a file with a library

To add an implementation file, put part *fileUri* in the file that has the library statement, where *fileUri* is the path to the implementation file. Then in the implementation file, put part of *identifier*, where *identifier* is the name of the library. The following example uses part and part of to implement a library in three files.

The first file, `ballgame.dart`, declares the ballgame library, imports other libraries it needs, and specifies that `ball.dart` and `util.dart` are parts of this library:

```
library ballgame;

import 'dart:html';
// ...Other imports go here...

part 'ball.dart';
part 'util.dart';

// ...Code might go here...
```

The second file, `ball.dart`, implements part of the ballgame library:

```
part of ballgame;

// ...Code goes here...
```

The third file, `util.dart`, implements the rest of the ballgame library:

```
part of ballgame;

// ...Code goes here...
```

Re-exporting libraries

You can combine or repackage libraries by re-exporting part or all of them. For example, you might have a huge library that you implement as a set of smaller libraries. Or you might create a library that provides a subset of methods from another library:

```
// In french.dart:
library french;
hello() => print('Bonjour!');
goodbye() => print('Au Revoir!');

// In togo.dart:
library togo;
import 'french.dart';
export 'french.dart' show hello;

// In another .dart file:
import 'togo.dart';

void main() {
  hello();   //print bonjour
  goodbye(); //FAIL
}
```

Isolates

Modern web browsers, even on mobile platforms, run on multi-core CPUs. To take advantage of all those cores, developers traditionally use shared-memory threads running concurrently. However, shared-state concurrency is error prone and can lead to complicated code.

Instead of threads, all Dart code runs inside of *isolates*. Each isolate has its own memory heap, ensuring that no isolate's state is accessible from any other isolate.

Typedefs

In Dart, functions are objects, just like strings and numbers are objects. A *typedef*, or *function-type alias*, gives a function type a name that you can use when declaring fields and return types. A typedef retains type information when a function type is assigned to a variable.

Consider the following code, which does not use a typedef:

```
class SortedCollection {
  Function compare;

  SortedCollection(int f(Object a, Object b)) {
    compare = f;
  }
}

int sort(Object a, Object b) => ... ; // Initial, broken implementation.

main() {
  SortedCollection collection = new SortedCollection(sort);

  // All we know is that compare is a function, but what type of function?
  assert(collection.compare is Function);
}
```

Type information is lost when assigning f to compare. The type of f is (Object, Object)→int (where → means returns), yet the type of compare is Function. If we change the code to use explicit names and retain type information, both developers and tools can use that information:

```
typedef int Compare(Object a, Object b);

class SortedCollection {
  Compare compare;

  SortedCollection(this.compare);
}
```

```
int sort(Object a, Object b) => ... ; // Initial, broken implementation.

main() {
  SortedCollection collection = new SortedCollection(sort);
  assert(collection.compare is Function);
  assert(collection.compare is Compare);
}
```

 Currently, typedefs are restricted to function types. We expect this to change.

Because typedefs are simply aliases, they offer a way to check the type of any function. For example:

```
typedef int Compare(int a, int b);

int sort(int a, int b) => a - b;

main() {
  assert(sort is Compare);  // True!
}
```

Metadata

Use metadata to give additional information about your code. A metadata annotation begins with the character @, followed by either a reference to a compile-time constant (such as deprecated) or a call to a constant constructor.

Three annotations are available to all Dart code: @deprecated, @override, and @proxy. For examples of using @override and @proxy, see "Extending a Class" on page 48. Here's an example of using the @deprecated annotation:

```
class Television {
  /// _Deprecated: Use [turnOn] instead._
  @deprecated      // Metadata; makes Dart Editor warn about using activate().
  void activate() {
    turnOn();
  }

  /// Turns the TV's power on.
  void turnOn() {
    print('on!');
  }
}
```

You can define your own metadata annotations. Here's an example of defining a @todo annotation that takes two arguments:

```
library todo;

class todo {
  final String who;
  final String what;

  const todo(this.who, this.what);
}
```

And here's an example of using that @todo annotation:

```
import 'todo.dart';

@todo('seth', 'make this do something')
void doSomething() {
  print('do something');
}
```

Metadata can appear before a library, class, typedef, type parameter, constructor, factory, function, field, parameter, or variable declaration and before an import or export directive. If issue #6614[26] is fixed by the time you read this, you can retrieve metadata at runtime using reflection.

Comments

Dart supports single-line comments, multi-line comments, and documentation comments.

Single-Line Comments

A single-line comment begins with //. Everything between // and the end of line is ignored by the Dart compiler.

```
main() {
  // TODO: refactor into an AbstractLlamaGreetingFactory?
  print('Welcome to my Llama farm!');
}
```

Multi-Line Comments

A multi-line comment begins with /* and ends with */. Everything between /* and */ is ignored by the Dart compiler (unless the comment is a documentation comment; see the next section). Multi-line comments can nest.

---

26. *https://code.google.com/p/dart/issues/detail?id=6614*

```
main() {
  /*
   * This is a lot of work. Consider raising chickens.

  Llama larry = new Llama();
  larry.feed();
  larry.exercise();
  larry.clean();
   */
}
```

Documentation Comments

Documentation comments are multi-line or single-line comments that begin with /** or ///. Using /// on consecutive lines has the same effect as a multi-line doc comment.

Inside a documentation comment, the Dart compiler ignores all text unless it is enclosed in brackets. Using brackets, you can refer to classes, methods, fields, top-level variables, functions, and parameters. The names in brackets are resolved in the lexical scope of the documented program element.

Here is an example of documentation comments with references to other classes and arguments:

```
/**
 * A domesticated South American camelid (Lama glama).
 *
 * Andean cultures have used llamas as meat and pack animals
 * since pre-Hispanic times.
 */
class Llama {
  String name;

  /**
   * Feeds your llama [Food].
   *
   * The typical llama eats one bale of hay per week.
   */
  void feed(Food food) {
    // ...
  }

  /// Exercises your llama with an [activity] for
  /// [timeLimit] minutes.
  void exercise(Activity activity, int timeLimit) {
    // ...
  }
}
```

In the generated documentation, [Food] becomes a link to the API docs for the Food class.

To parse Dart code and generate HTML documentation, you can use the SDK's documentation generation tool. For an example of generated documentation, see the Dart API documentation.[27] For advice on how to structure your comments, see Guidelines for Dart Doc Comments.[28]

Summary

This chapter summarized the commonly used features in the Dart language. More features are being implemented,[29] but we expect that they won't break existing code. For more information, see the Dart Language Specification[30] and articles[31] such as "Idiomatic Dart[32]."

---

27. *http://api.dartlang.org*

28. *http://www.dartlang.org/articles/doc-comment-guidelines/*

29. *http://www.dartlang.org/articles/mixins/*

30. *http://www.dartlang.org/docs/spec/*

31. *http://www.dartlang.org/articles/*

32. *http://www.dartlang.org/articles/idiomatic-dart/*

CHAPTER 3

A Tour of the Dart Libraries

This chapter shows you how to use the major features in Dart's libraries. It's just an overview, and by no means comprehensive. Whenever you need more details about a class, consult the Dart API reference.[1]

dart:core—Numbers, Collections, Strings, and More

The Dart core library provides a small but critical set of built-in functionality. This library is automatically imported into every Dart program.

Numbers

The dart:core library defines the num, int, and double classes, which have some basic utilities for working with numbers.

You can convert a string into an integer or double with the `parse()` methods of int and double, respectively:

```
assert(int.parse('42') == 42);
assert(int.parse('0x42') == 66);
assert(double.parse('0.50') == 0.5);
```

Or use the parse() method of num, which creates an integer if possible and otherwise a double:

```
assert(num.parse('42') is int);
assert(num.parse('0x42') is int);
assert(num.parse('0.50') is double);
```

To specify the base of an integer, add a `radix` parameter:

---

1. *http://api.dartlang.org/*

```
assert(int.parse('42', radix: 16) == 66);
```

Use the `toString()` method (defined by Object[2]) to convert an int or double to a string. To specify the number of digits to the right of the decimal, use `toStringAsFixed()` (defined by num). To specify the number of significant digits in the string, use `toStringAsPrecision()` (also in num):

```
// Convert an int to a string.
assert(42.toString() == '42');

// Convert a double to a string.
assert(123.456.toString() == '123.456');

// Specify the number of digits after the decimal.
assert(123.456.toStringAsFixed(2) == '123.46');

// Specify the number of significant figures.
assert(123.456.toStringAsPrecision(2) == '1.2e+2');
assert(double.parse('1.2e+2') == 120.0);
```

For more information, see the API documentation for int,[3] double,[4] and num.[5] Also see "dart:math—Math and Random" on page 79.

Strings and Regular Expressions

A string in Dart is an immutable sequence of UTF-16 code units. The language tour has more information about strings (page 17). You can use regular expressions (RegExp objects) to search within strings and to replace parts of strings.

The String class defines such methods as `split()`, `contains()`, `startsWith()`, `endsWith()`, and more.

Searching inside a string

You can find particular locations within a string, as well as check whether a string begins with or ends with a particular pattern. For example:

```
// Check whether a string contains another string.
assert('Never odd or even'.contains('odd'));

// Does a string start with another string?
assert('Never odd or even'.startsWith('Never'));

// Does a string end with another string?
```

2. *http://api.dartlang.org/dart_core/Object.html*
3. *http://api.dartlang.org/dart_core/int.html*
4. *http://api.dartlang.org/dart_core/double.html*
5. *http://api.dartlang.org/dart_core/num.html*

```
assert('Never odd or even'.endsWith('even'));

// Find the location of a string inside a string.
assert('Never odd or even'.indexOf('odd') == 6);
```

Extracting data from a string

You can get the individual characters from a string as Strings or ints, respectively. To be precise, you actually get individual UTF-16 code units; high-numbered characters such as the treble clef symbol ('\u{1D11E}') are two code units apiece.

You can also extract a substring or split a string into a list of substrings:

```
// Grab a substring.
assert('Never odd or even'.substring(6, 9) == 'odd');

// Split a string using a string pattern.
var parts = 'structured web apps'.split(' ');
assert(parts.length == 3);
assert(parts[0] == 'structured');

// Get a UTF-16 code unit (as a string) by index.
assert('Never odd or even'[0] == 'N');

// Use split() with an empty string parameter to get a list of
// all code units (as Strings); good for iterating.
for (var char in 'hello'.split('')) {
  print(char);
}

// Get all the UTF-16 code units in the string.
var codeUnitList = 'Never odd or even'.codeUnits.toList();
assert(codeUnitList[0] == 78);
```

Converting to uppercase or lowercase

You can easily convert strings to their uppercase and lowercase variants:

```
// Convert to uppercase.
assert('structured web apps'.toUpperCase() == 'STRUCTURED WEB APPS');

// Convert to lowercase.
assert('STRUCTURED WEB APPS'.toLowerCase() == 'structured web apps');
```

 These methods don't work for every language. For example, the Turkish alphabet's dotless *I* is converted incorrectly.

Trimming and empty strings

Remove all leading and trailing white space with trim(). To check whether a string is empty (length is zero), use isEmpty:

```
// Trim a string.
assert(' hello '.trim() == 'hello');

// Check whether a string is empty.
assert(''.isEmpty);

// Strings with only white space are not empty.
assert(!' '.isEmpty);
```

Replacing part of a string

Strings are immutable objects, which means you can create them but you can't change them. If you look closely at the String API docs,[6] you'll notice that none of the methods actually changes the state of a String. For example, the method replaceAll() returns a new String without changing the original String:

```
var greetingTemplate = 'Hello, NAME!';
var greeting = greetingTemplate.replaceAll(new RegExp('NAME'), 'Bob');

assert(greeting != greetingTemplate); // greetingTemplate didn't change.
```

Building a string

To programmatically generate a string, you can use StringBuffer. A StringBuffer doesn't generate a new String object until toString() is called. The writeAll() method has an optional second parameter that lets you specify a separator—in this case, a space:

```
var sb = new StringBuffer();

sb..write('Use a StringBuffer ')
  ..writeAll(['for', 'efficient', 'string', 'creation'], ' ')
  ..write('.');

var fullString = sb.toString();

assert(fullString ==
    'Use a StringBuffer for efficient string creation.');
```

Regular expressions

The RegExp class provides the same capabilities as JavaScript regular expressions. Use regular expressions for efficient searching and pattern matching of strings:

---

6. *http://api.dartlang.org/dart_core/String.html*

```
// Here's a regular expression for one or more digits.
var numbers = new RegExp(r'\d+');

var allCharacters = 'llamas live fifteen to twenty years';
var someDigits = 'llamas live 15 to 20 years';

// contains() can use a regular expression.
assert(!allCharacters.contains(numbers));
assert(someDigits.contains(numbers));

// Replace every match with another string.
var exedOut = someDigits.replaceAll(numbers, 'XX');
assert(exedOut == 'llamas live XX to XX years');
```

You can work directly with the RegExp class, too. The Match class provides access to a regular expression match:

```
var numbers = new RegExp(r'\d+');
var someDigits = 'llamas live 15 to 20 years';

// Check whether the reg exp has a match in a string.
assert(numbers.hasMatch(someDigits));

// Loop through all matches.
for (var match in numbers.allMatches(someDigits)) {
  print(match.group(0)); // 15, then 20
}
```

More information

Refer to the String API docs[7] for a full list of methods. Also see the API docs for String-Buffer[8], Pattern[9], RegExp[10], and Match[11].

Collections

Dart ships with a core collections API, which includes classes for lists, sets, and maps.

Lists

As the language tour shows, you can use literals to create and initialize lists (page 20). Alternatively, use one of the List constructors. The List class also defines several methods for adding items to and removing items from lists:

---

7. *http://api.dartlang.org/dart_core/String.html*

8. *http://api.dartlang.org/dart_core/StringBuffer.html*

9. *http://api.dartlang.org/dart_core/Pattern.html*

10. *http://api.dartlang.org/dart_core/RegExp.html*

11. *http://api.dartlang.org/dart_core/Match.html*

```
// Use a List constructor.
var vegetables = new List();

// Or simply use a list literal.
var fruits = ['apples', 'oranges'];

// Add to a list.
fruits.add('kiwis');

// Add multiple items to a list.
fruits.addAll(['grapes', 'bananas']);

// Get the list length.
assert(fruits.length == 5);

// Remove a single item.
var appleIndex = fruits.indexOf('apples');
fruits.removeAt(appleIndex);
assert(fruits.length == 4);

// Remove all elements from a list.
fruits.clear();
assert(fruits.length == 0);
```

Use indexOf() to find the index of an object in a list:

```
var fruits = ['apples', 'oranges'];

// Access a list item by index.
assert(fruits[0] == 'apples');

// Find an item in a list.
assert(fruits.indexOf('apples') == 0);
```

Sort a list using the sort() method. You can provide a sorting function that compares two objects. This sorting function must return < 0 for *smaller*, 0 for the *same*, and > 0 for *bigger*. The following example uses compareTo(), which is defined by Comparable[12] and implemented by String:

```
var fruits = ['bananas', 'apples', 'oranges'];

// Sort a list.
fruits.sort((a, b) => a.compareTo(b));
assert(fruits[0] == 'apples');
```

Lists are parameterized types, so you can specify the type that a list should contain:

```
// This list should contain only strings.
var fruits = new List<String>();
```

12. *http://api.dartlang.org/dart_core/Comparable.html*

```
fruits.add('apples');
var fruit = fruits[0];
assert(fruit is String);

// Generates static analysis warning, num is not a string.
fruits.add(5);  // BAD: Throws exception in checked mode.
```

Refer to the List API docs[13] for a full list of methods.

Sets

A set in Dart is an unordered collection of unique items. Because a set is unordered, you can't get a set's items by index (position):

```
var ingredients = new Set();
ingredients.addAll(['gold', 'titanium', 'xenon']);
assert(ingredients.length == 3);

// Adding a duplicate item has no effect.
ingredients.add('gold');
assert(ingredients.length == 3);

// Remove an item from a set.
ingredients.remove('gold');
assert(ingredients.length == 2);
```

Use contains() and containsAll() to check whether one or more objects are in a set:

```
var ingredients = new Set();
ingredients.addAll(['gold', 'titanium', 'xenon']);

// Check whether an item is in the set.
assert(ingredients.contains('titanium'));

// Check whether all the items are in the set.
assert(ingredients.containsAll(['titanium', 'xenon']));
```

An intersection is a set whose items are in two other sets:

```
var ingredients = new Set();
ingredients.addAll(['gold', 'titanium', 'xenon']);

// Create the intersection of two sets.
var nobleGases = new Set.from(['xenon', 'argon']);
var intersection = ingredients.intersection(nobleGases);
assert(intersection.length == 1);
assert(intersection.contains('xenon'));
```

Refer to the Set API docs[14] for a full list of methods.

---

13. *http://api.dartlang.org/dart_core/List.html*
14. *http://api.dartlang.org/dart_core/Set.html*

```
```

Maps

A map, commonly known as a *dictionary* or *hash*, is an unordered collection of key-value pairs. Maps associate a key to some value for easy retrieval. Unlike in JavaScript, Dart objects are not maps.

You can declare a map using a terse literal syntax, or you can use a traditional constructor:

```
// Maps often use strings as keys.
var hawaiianBeaches = {
  'oahu'       : ['waikiki', 'kailua', 'waimanalo'],
  'big island' : ['wailea bay', 'pololu beach'],
  'kauai'      : ['hanalei', 'poipu']
};

// Maps can be built from a constructor.
var searchTerms = new Map();

// Maps are parameterized types; you can specify what types
// the key and value should be.
var nobleGases = new Map<int, String>();
```

You add, get, and set map items using the bracket syntax. Use remove() to remove a key and its value from a map:

```
var nobleGases = { 54: 'xenon' };

// Retrieve a value with a key.
assert(nobleGases[54] == 'xenon');

// Check whether a map contains a key.
assert(nobleGases.containsKey(54));

// Remove a key and its value.
nobleGases.remove(54);
assert(!nobleGases.containsKey(54));
```

You can retrieve all the values or all the keys from a map:

```
var hawaiianBeaches = {
  'oahu' : ['waikiki', 'kailua', 'waimanalo'],
  'big island' : ['wailea bay', 'pololu beach'],
  'kauai' : ['hanalei', 'poipu']
};

// Get all the keys as an unordered collection (an Iterable).
var keys = hawaiianBeaches.keys;

assert(keys.length == 3);
assert(new Set.from(keys).contains('oahu'));

// Get all the values as an unordered collection (an Iterable of Lists).
var values = hawaiianBeaches.values;
```

```
assert(values.length == 3);
assert(values.any((v) => v.contains('waikiki')));
```

To check whether a map contains a key, use containsKey(). Because map values can be null, you cannot rely on simply getting the value for the key and checking for null to determine the existence of a key:

```
var hawaiianBeaches = {
  'oahu' : ['waikiki', 'kailua', 'waimanalo'],
  'big island' : ['wailea bay', 'pololu beach'],
  'kauai' : ['hanalei', 'poipu']
};

assert(hawaiianBeaches.containsKey('oahu'));
assert(!hawaiianBeaches.containsKey('florida'));
```

Use the putIfAbsent() method when you want to assign a value to a key if and only if the key does not already exist in a map. You must provide a function that returns the value:

```
var teamAssignments = {};
teamAssignments.putIfAbsent('Catcher', () => pickToughestKid());
assert(teamAssignments['Catcher'] != null);
```

Refer to the Map API docs[15] for a full list of methods.

Common collection methods

List, Set, and Map share common functionality found in many collections. Some of this common functionality is defined by the Iterable class, which List and Set implement.

Although Map doesn't implement Iterable, you can get Iterables from it using the Map keys and values properties.

Use isEmpty to check whether a list, set, or map has no items:

```
var teas = ['green', 'black', 'chamomile', 'earl grey'];
assert(!teas.isEmpty);
```

To apply a function to each item in a list, set, or map, you can use forEach():

```
var teas = ['green', 'black', 'chamomile', 'earl grey'];

teas.forEach((tea) => print('I drink $tea'));
```

---

15. *http://api.dartlang.org/dart_core/Map.html*

When you invoke forEach() on a map, your function must take two arguments (the key and value):

```
hawaiianBeaches.forEach((k, v) {
  print('I want to visit $k and swim at $v');
  // I want to visit oahu and swim at [waikiki, kailua, waimanalo], etc.
});
```

Iterables provide the map() method, which gives you all the results in a single object:

```
var teas = ['green', 'black', 'chamomile', 'earl grey'];

var loudTeas = teas.map((tea) => tea.toUpperCase());
loudTeas.forEach(print);
```

 The object returned by map() is an Iterable that's *lazily evaluated*: your function isn't called until you ask for an item from the returned object.

To force your function to be called immediately on each item, use map().toList() or map().toSet():

```
var loudTeaList = teas.map((tea) => tea.toUpperCase()).toList();
```

Use Iterable's where() method to get all the items that match a condition. Use Iterable's any() and every() methods to check whether some or all items match a condition:

```
var teas = ['green', 'black', 'chamomile', 'earl grey'];

// Chamomile is not caffeinated.
bool isDecaffeinated(String teaName) => teaName == 'chamomile';

// Use where() to find only the items that return true
// from the provided function.
var decaffeinatedTeas = teas.where((tea) => isDecaffeinated(tea));
// or teas.where(isDecaffeinated)

// Use any() to check whether at least one item in the collection
// satisfies a condition.
assert(teas.any(isDecaffeinated));

// Use every() to check whether all the items in a collection
// satisfy a condition.
assert(!teas.every(isDecaffeinated));
```

For a full list of methods, refer to the Iterable API docs,[16] as well as those for List, Set, and Map.

16. *http://api.dartlang.org/dart_core/Iterable.html*

URIs

The Uri class[17] provides functions to encode and decode strings for use in URIs (which you might know as *URLs*). These functions handle characters that are special for URIs, such as & and =. The Uri class also parses and exposes the components of a URI—host, port, scheme, and so on.

Encoding and decoding fully qualified URIs

To encode and decode characters *except* those with special meaning in a URI (such as /, :, &, #), use the encodeFull() and decodeFull() methods. These methods are good for encoding or decoding a fully qualified URI, leaving intact special URI characters:

```
main() {
  var uri = 'http://example.org/api?foo=some message';
  var encoded = Uri.encodeFull(uri);
  assert(encoded == 'http://example.org/api?foo=some%20message');

  var decoded = Uri.decodeFull(encoded);
  assert(uri == decoded);
}
```

Notice how only the space between some and message was encoded.

Encoding and decoding URI components

To encode and decode all of a string's characters that have special meaning in a URI, including (but not limited to) /, &, and :, use the encodeComponent() and decodeComponent() methods:

```
main() {
  var uri = 'http://example.org/api?foo=some message';
  var encoded = Uri.encodeComponent(uri);
  assert(encoded == 'http%3A%2F%2Fexample.org%2Fapi%3Ffoo%3Dsome%20message');

  var decoded = Uri.decodeComponent(encoded);
  assert(uri == decoded);
}
```

Notice how every special character is encoded. For example, / is encoded to %2F.

Parsing URIs

If you have a Uri object or a URI string, you can get its parts using Uri fields such as path. To create a Uri from a string, use the parse() static method:

```
main() {
  var uri = Uri.parse('http://example.org:8080/foo/bar#frag');
```

---

17. *http://api.dartlang.org/dart_core/Uri.html*

```
    assert(uri.scheme   == 'http');
    assert(uri.host     == 'example.org');
    assert(uri.path     == '/foo/bar');
    assert(uri.fragment == 'frag');
    assert(uri.origin   == 'http://example.org:8080');
}
```

See the Uri API docs[18] for more URI components that you can get.

Building URIs

You can build up a URI from individual parts using the Uri() constructor:

```
main() {
  var uri = new Uri(scheme: 'http', host: 'example.org',
                    path: '/foo/bar', fragment: 'frag');
  assert(uri.toString() == 'http://example.org/foo/bar#frag');
}
```

Dates and Times

A DateTime object is a point in time. The time zone is either UTC or the local time zone.

You can create DateTime objects using several constructors:

```
// Get the current date and time.
var now = new DateTime.now();

// Create a new DateTime with the local time zone.
var y2k = new DateTime(2000);    // January 1, 2000

// Specify the month and day.
y2k = new DateTime(2000, 1, 2); // January 2, 2000

// Specify the date as a UTC time.
y2k = new DateTime.utc(2000);    // January 1, 2000, UTC

// Specify a date and time in milliseconds since the Unix epoch.
y2k = new DateTime.fromMillisecondsSinceEpoch(946684800000, isUtc: true);

// Parse an ISO 8601 date.
y2k = DateTime.parse('2000-01-01T00:00:00Z');
```

The millisecondsSinceEpoch property of a date returns the number of milliseconds since the "Unix epoch"—January 1, 1970, UTC:

```
var y2k = new DateTime.utc(2000);            // 1/1/2000, UTC
assert(y2k.millisecondsSinceEpoch == 946684800000);
```

18. *http://api.dartlang.org/dart_core/Uri.html*

```
var unixEpoch = new DateTime.utc(1970); // 1/1/1970, UTC
assert(unixEpoch.millisecondsSinceEpoch == 0);
```

Use the Duration class to calculate the difference between two dates and to shift a date forward or backward:

```
var y2k = new DateTime.utc(2000);

// Add one year.
var y2001 = y2k.add(const Duration(days: 366));
assert(y2001.year == 2001);

// Subtract 30 days.
var december2000 = y2001.subtract(const Duration(days: 30));
assert(december2000.year == 2000);
assert(december2000.month == 12);

// Calculate the difference between two dates.
// Returns a Duration object.
var duration = y2001.difference(y2k);
assert(duration.inDays == 366); // y2k was a leap year.
```

Using a Duration to shift a DateTime by days can be problematic, due to clock shifts (to Daylight Savings Time, for example). Use UTC dates if you must shift days.

Refer to the API docs for DateTime[19] and Duration[20] for a full list of methods.

Utility Classes

The core library contains various utility classes, useful for sorting, mapping values, and iterating.

Comparing objects

Implement the Comparable[21] interface to indicate that an object can be compared to another object, usually for sorting. The compareTo() method returns < 0 for *smaller*, 0 for the *same*, and > 0 for *bigger*:

```
class Line implements Comparable {
  final length;
  const Line(this.length);
  int compareTo(Line other) => length - other.length;
```

---

19. *http://api.dartlang.org/dart_core/DateTime.html*

20. *http://api.dartlang.org/dart_core/Duration.html*

21. *http://api.dartlang.org/dart_core/Comparable.html*

```
  }
main() {
  var short = const Line(1);
  var long = const Line(100);
  assert(short.compareTo(long) < 0);
}
```

Implementing map keys

Each object in Dart automatically provides an integer hash code, and thus can be used as a key in a map. However, you can override the hashCode getter to generate a custom hash code. If you do, you might also want to override the == operator. Objects that are equal (via ==) must have identical hash codes. A hash code doesn't have to be unique, but it should be well distributed:

```
class Person {
  final String firstName, lastName;

  Person(this.firstName, this.lastName);

  // Override hashCode using strategy from Effective Java, Chapter 11.
  int get hashCode {
    int result = 17;
    result = 37 * result + firstName.hashCode;
    result = 37 * result + lastName.hashCode;
    return result;
  }

  // You should generally implement operator== if you override hashCode.
  bool operator==(other) {
    if (other is! Person) return false;
    Person person = other;
    return (person.firstName == firstName && person.lastName == lastName);
  }
}

main() {
  var p1 = new Person('bob', 'smith');
  var p2 = new Person('bob', 'smith');
  var p3 = 'not a person';
  assert(p1.hashCode == p2.hashCode);
  assert(p1 == p2);
  assert(p1 != p3);
}
```

Iteration

The Iterable[22] and Iterator[23] classes support for-in loops. Extend (if possible) or implement Iterable whenever you create a class that can provide Iterators for use in for-in loops. Implement Iterator to define the actual iteration ability:

```dart
class Process {
  // Represents a process...
}

class ProcessIterator implements Iterator<Process> {
  Process current;
  bool moveNext() {
    return false;
  }
}

// A mythical class that lets you iterate through all processes.
// Extends a subclass of Iterable.
class Processes extends IterableBase<Process> {
  final Iterator<Process> iterator = new ProcessIterator();
}

main() {
  // Iterable objects can be used with for-in.
  for (var process in new Processes()) {
    // Do something with the process.
  }
}
```

Exceptions

The Dart core library defines many common exceptions and errors. Exceptions are considered conditions that you can plan ahead for and catch. Errors are conditions that you don't expect or plan for.

A couple of the most common errors are:

NoSuchMethodError[24]

Thrown when a receiving object (which might be null) does not implement a method.

ArgumentError[25]

Can be thrown by a method that encounters an unexpected argument.

---

22. *http://api.dartlang.org/dart_core/Iterable.html*

23. *http://api.dartlang.org/dart_core/Iterator.html*

24. *http://api.dartlang.org/dart_core/NoSuchMethodError.html*

25. *http://api.dartlang.org/dart_core/ArgumentError.html*

Throwing an application-specific exception is a common way to indicate that an error has occurred. You can define a custom exception by implementing the Exception interface:

```
class FooException implements Exception {
  final String msg;
  const FooException([this.msg]);
  String toString() => msg == null ? 'FooException' : msg;
}
```

For more information, see "Exceptions" on page 36 and the Exception API docs.[26]

dart:async—Asynchronous Programming

Asynchronous programming often uses callback functions, but Dart provides alternatives: Future[27] and Stream[28] objects. A Future is like a promise for a result to be provided sometime in the future. A Stream is a way to get a sequence of values, such as events. Future, Stream, and more are in the dart:async[29] library.

The dart:async library works in both web apps and command-line apps. To use it, import dart:async:

```
import 'dart:async';
```

Future

Future objects appear throughout the Dart libraries, often as the object returned by an asynchronous method. When a future *completes*, its value is ready to use.

Basic usage

Use then() to schedule code that runs when the future completes. For example, HttpRequest.getString() returns a Future, since HTTP requests can take a while. Using then() lets you run some code when that Future has completed and the promised string value is available:

```
HttpRequest.getString(url)
  .then((String result) {
    print(result); });
  // Should handle errors here
```

Use catchError() to handle any errors or exceptions that a Future object might throw:

---

26. *http://api.dartlang.org/dart_core/Exception.html*
27. *http://api.dartlang.org/dart_async/Future.html*
28. *http://api.dartlang.org/dart_async/Stream.html*
29. *http://api.dartlang.org/dart_async.html*

```
HttpRequest.getString(url)
  .then((String result) {  // callback function
    print(result); })
  .catchError((e) {
    // Handle or ignore the error.
  });
```

The then().catchError() pattern is the asynchronous version of try-catch.

 Be sure to invoke catchError() on the result of then()—not on the result of the original Future. Otherwise, the catchError() can handle errors only from the original Future's computation, but not from the handler registered by then().

Chaining multiple asynchronous methods

The then() method returns a Future, providing a useful way to run multiple asynchronous functions in a certain order. If the callback registered with then() returns a Future, then() returns an equivalent Future. If the callback returns a value of any other type, then() creates a new Future that completes with the value:

```
Future result = costlyQuery();

return result.then((value) => expensiveWork())
             .then((value) => lengthyComputation())
             .then((value) => print('done!'))
             .catchError((exception) => print('DOH!'));
```

In the preceding example, the methods run in the following order:

1. costlyQuery()

2. expensiveWork()

3. lengthyComputation()

Waiting for multiple Futures

Sometimes your algorithm needs to invoke many asynchronous functions and wait for them all to complete before continuing. Use the Future.wait()[30] static method to manage multiple Futures and wait for them to complete:

```
Future deleteDone = deleteLotsOfFiles();
Future copyDone = copyLotsOfFiles();
Future checksumDone = checksumLotsOfOtherFiles();
```

---

30. *http://api.dartlang.org/dart_async/Future.html#wait*

```
Future.wait([deleteDone, copyDone, checksumDone]).then((List values) {
  print('Done with all the long steps');
});
```

Stream

Stream objects appear throughout Dart APIs, representing sequences of data. For example, HTML events such as button clicks are delivered using streams. You can also read a file as a stream.

Listening for stream data

To get each value as it arrives, subscribe to the stream using the listen() method:

```
// Find a button by ID and add an event handler.
querySelector('#submitInfo').onClick.listen((e) {
  // When the button is clicked, it runs this code.
  submitData();
});
```

In this example, the onClick property is a stream object provided by the 'submitInfo' button.

If you care about only one event, you can get it using a property such as first, last, or single. To test the event before handling it, use a method such as firstWhere(), lastWhere(), or singleWhere().

If you care about a subset of events, you can use methods such as skip(), skipWhile(), take(), takeWhile(), and where().

Transforming stream data

Often, you need to change the format of a stream's data before you can use it. Use the transform() method to produce a stream with a different type of data:

```
var config = new File('config.txt');
Stream<List<int>> inputStream = config.openRead();

inputStream
  .transform(UTF8.decoder)
  .transform(new LineSplitter())
  .listen(
    (String line) {...} ...);
```

This example uses two transformers. First it uses UTF8.decoder to transform the stream of integers into a stream of strings. Then it uses a LineSplitter to transform the stream of strings into a stream of separate lines. These transformers are from the dart:convert library (see "dart:convert—Decoding and Encoding JSON, UTF-8, and More" on page 96).

More Information

For some examples of using Future and Stream in command-line apps, see "dart:io—I/O for Command-Line Apps" on page 90. Also see these articles and tutorials:

- Use Future-Based APIs[31]
- Futures and Error Handling[32]
- The Event Loop and Dart[33]
- Use Streams for Data[34]
- Creating Streams in Dart[35]

dart:math—Math and Random

The Math library provides common functionality such as sine and cosine, maximum and minimum, and constants such as *pi* and *e*. Most of the functionality in the Math library is implemented as top-level functions.

To use the Math library in your app, import dart:math. The following examples use the prefix `math` to make clear which top-level functions and constants are from the Math library:

```
import 'dart:math' as math;
```

Trigonometry

The Math library provides basic trigonometric functions:

```
// Cosine
assert(math.cos(math.PI) == -1.0);

// Sine
var degrees = 30;
var radians = degrees * (math.PI / 180);
// radians is now 0.52359.
var sinOf30degrees = math.sin(radians);

// Truncate the decimal places to 2.
assert(double.parse(sinOf30degrees.toStringAsPrecision(2)) == 0.5);
```

31. *http://www.dartlang.org/docs/tutorials/futures/*
32. *http://www.dartlang.org/articles/futures-and-error-handling/*
33. *http://www.dartlang.org/articles/event-loop/*
34. *https://www.dartlang.org/docs/tutorials/streams/*
35. *http://www.dartlang.org/articles/creating-streams/*

These functions use radians, not degrees!

Maximum and Minimum

The Math library provides max() and min() methods:

```
assert(math.max(1, 1000) == 1000);
assert(math.min(1, -1000) == -1000);
```

Math Constants

Find your favorite constants—*pi*, *e*, and more—in the Math library:

```
// See the Math library for additional constants.
print(math.E);    // 2.718281828459045
print(math.PI);   // 3.141592653589793
print(math.SQRT2); // 1.4142135623730951
```

Random Numbers

Generate random numbers with the Random[36] class. You can optionally provide a seed to the Random constructor:

```
var random = new math.Random();
random.nextDouble(); // Between 0.0 and 1.0: [0, 1)
random.nextInt(10);  // Between 0 and 9.
```

You can even generate random booleans:

```
var random = new math.Random();
random.nextBool();  // true or false
```

More Information

Refer to the Math API docs[37] for a full list of methods. Also see the API docs for num,[38] int,[39] and double.[40]

36. *http://api.dartlang.org/dart_math/Random.html*

37. *http://api.dartlang.org/dart_math/index.html*

38. *http://api.dartlang.org/dart_core/num.html*

39. *http://api.dartlang.org/dart_core/int.html*

40. *http://api.dartlang.org/dart_core/double.html*

dart:html—Browser-Based Apps

Use the dart:html library[41] to program the browser, manipulate objects and elements in the DOM, and access HTML5 APIs. *DOM* stands for *Document Object Model*, which describes the hierarchy of an HTML page.

Other common uses of dart:html are manipulating styles (*CSS*), getting data using HTTP requests, and exchanging data using WebSockets (page 88). HTML5 (and dart:html) has many additional APIs that this section doesn't cover. Only web apps can use dart:html, not command-line apps.

For higher level approaches to web app UIs, see Polymer.dart[42] and AngularDart[43].

To use the HTML library in your web app, import dart:html:

```
import 'dart:html';
```

Parts of the dart:html library are experimental, as noted in the API documentation.

Manipulating the DOM

To use the DOM, you need to know about *windows*, *documents*, *elements*, and *nodes*.

A Window[44] object represents the actual window of the web browser. Each Window has a Document object, which points to the document that's currently loaded. The Window object also has accessors to various APIs such as IndexedDB (for storing data), requestAnimationFrame (for animations), and more. In tabbed browsers, each tab has its own Window object.

With the Document[45] object, you can create and manipulate Elements[46] within the document. Note that the document itself is an element and can be manipulated.

---

41. *http://api.dartlang.org/dart_html.html*
42. *http://www.dartlang.org/polymer-dart/*
43. *http://pub.dartlang.org/packages/angular*
44. *http://api.dartlang.org/html/Window.html*
45. *http://api.dartlang.org/html/Document.html*
46. *http://api.dartlang.org/html/Element.html*

The DOM models a tree of Nodes.[47] These nodes are often elements, but they can also be attributes, text, comments, and other DOM types. Except for the root node, which has no parent, each node in the DOM has one parent and might have many children.

Finding elements

To manipulate an element, you first need an object that represents it. You can get this object using a query.

Find one or more elements using the top-level functions querySelector() and querySelectorAll(). You can query by ID, class, tag, name, or any combination of these. The CSS Selector Specification guide[48] defines the formats of the selectors such as using a # prefix to specify IDs and a period (.) for classes.

The querySelector() function returns the first element that matches the selector, while querySelectorAll() returns a collection of elements that match the selector:

```
Element elem1 = querySelector('#an-id');
// Find an element by id (an-id).
Element elem2 = querySelector('.a-class');
// Find an element by class (a-class).
List<Element> elems1 = querySelectorAll('div');
// Find all elements by tag (<div>).
List<Element> elems2 = querySelectorAll('input[type="text"]');
// Find all text inputs.

// Find all elements with the CSS class 'class' inside of a <p>
// that is inside an element with the ID 'id'.
List<Element> elems3 = querySelectorAll('#id p.class');
```

Manipulating elements

You can use properties to change the state of an element. Node and its subtype Element define the properties that all elements have. For example, all elements have classes, hidden, id, style, and title properties that you can use to set state. Subclasses of Element define additional properties, such as the href property of AnchorElement.[49]

Consider this example of specifying an anchor element in HTML:

```
<a id="example" href="http://example.com">link text</a>
```

This <a> tag specifies an element with an href attribute and a text node (accessible via a text property) that contains the string "linktext". To change the URL that the link goes to, you can use AnchorElement's href property:

```
querySelector('#example').href = 'http://dartlang.org';
```

---

47. *http://api.dartlang.org/html/Node.html*
48. *http://www.w3.org/TR/css3-selectors/*
49. *http://api.dartlang.org/html/AnchorElement.html*

Often you need to set properties on multiple elements. For example, the following code sets the hidden property of all elements that have a class of "mac", "win", or "linux". Setting the hidden property to true has the same effect as adding display:none to the CSS:

```
<!-- In HTML: -->
<p>
  <span class="os linux">Words for Linux</span>
  <span class="os mac">Words for Mac</span>
  <span class="os win">Words for Windows</span>
</p>
// In Dart:
final osList = ['mac', 'win', 'linux'];

var userOs = 'linux'; // In real code you'd programmatically determine this.

for (var os in osList) {            // For each possible OS...
  bool shouldShow = (os == userOs); // Does this OS match the user's OS?
  for (var elem in querySelectorAll('.$os')) { // Find all elements for this OS.
    elem.hidden = !shouldShow;      // Show or hide each element.
  }
}
```

When the right property isn't available or convenient, you can use Element's attributes property. This property is a Map<String, String>, where the keys are attribute names. For a list of attribute names and their meanings, see the MDN Attributes page.[50] Here's an example of setting an attribute's value:

```
elem.attributes['someAttribute'] = 'someValue';
```

Creating elements

You can add to existing HTML pages by creating new elements and attaching them to the DOM. Here's an example of creating a paragraph (<p>) element:

```
var elem = new ParagraphElement();
elem.text = 'Creating is easy!';
```

You can also create an element by parsing HTML text. Any child elements are also parsed and created:

```
var elem2 = new Element.html('<p>Creating <em>is</em> easy!</p>');
```

Note that elem2 is a ParagraphElement in the preceding example.

Attach the newly created element to the document by assigning a parent to the element. You can add an element to any existing element's children. In the following example, body is an element, and its child elements are accessible (as a List<Element>) from the children property:

---

50. *https://developer.mozilla.org/en/HTML/Attributes*

```
document.body.children.add(elem2);
```

Adding, replacing, and removing nodes

Recall that elements are just a kind of node. You can find all the children of a node using the nodes property of Node, which returns a List<Node> (as opposed to children, which omits non-Element nodes). Once you have this list, you can use the usual List methods and operators to manipulate the children of the node.

To add a node as the last child of its parent, use the List add() method:

```
// Find the parent by ID, and add elem as its last child.
querySelector('#inputs').nodes.add(elem);
```

To replace a node, use the Node replaceWith() method:

```
// Find a node by ID, and replace it in the DOM.
querySelector('#status').replaceWith(elem);
```

To remove a node, use the Node remove() method:

```
// Find a node by ID, and remove it from the DOM.
querySelector('#expendable').remove();
```

Manipulating CSS styles

CSS, or *cascading style sheets*, defines the presentation styles of DOM elements. You can change the appearance of an element by attaching ID and class attributes to it.

Each element has a classes field, which is a list. Add and remove CSS classes simply by adding and removing strings from this collection. For example, the following sample adds the warning class to an element:

```
var element = querySelector('#message');
element.classes.add('warning');
```

It's often very efficient to find an element by ID. You can dynamically set an element ID with the id property:

```
var message = new DivElement();
message.id = 'message2';
message.text = 'Please subscribe to the Dart mailing list.';
```

You can reduce the redundant text in this example by using method cascades:

```
var message = new DivElement()
    ..id = 'message2'
    ..text = 'Please subscribe to the Dart mailing list.';
```

While using IDs and classes to associate an element with a set of styles is best practice, sometimes you want to attach a specific style directly to the element:

```
message.style
    ..fontWeight = 'bold'
    ..fontSize = '3em';
```

Handling events

To respond to external events such as clicks, changes of focus, and selections, add an event listener. You can add an event listener to any element on the page. Event dispatch and propagation is a complicated subject; research the details[51] if you're new to web programming.

Add an event handler using `element.onEvent.listen(function)`, where *Event* is the event name and *function* is the event handler.

For example, here's how you can handle clicks on a button:

```
// Find a button by ID and add an event handler.
querySelector('#submitInfo').onClick.listen((e) {
  // When the button is clicked, it runs this code.
  submitData();
});
```

Events can propagate up and down through the DOM tree. To discover which element originally fired the event, use `e.target`:

```
document.body.onClick.listen((e) {
  var clickedElem = e.target;
  print('You clicked the ${clickedElem.id} element.');
});
```

To see all the events for which you can register an event listener, look for *onEventType* properties in the API docs for Element[52] and its subclasses. Some common events include:

- change
- blur
- keyDown
- keyUp
- mouseDown
- mouseUp

---

51. *http://www.w3.org/TR/DOM-Level-3-Events/#dom-event-architecture*

52. *http://api.dartlang.org/dart_html/Element.html*

Using HTTP Resources with HttpRequest

Formerly known as XMLHttpRequest, the HttpRequest[53] class gives you access to HTTP resources from within your browser-based app. Traditionally, AJAX-style apps make heavy use of HttpRequest. Use HttpRequest to dynamically load JSON data or any other resource from a web server. You can also dynamically send data to a web server.

The following examples assume all resources are served from the same web server that hosts the script itself. Due to security restrictions in the browser, the HttpRequest class can't easily use resources that are hosted on an origin that is different from the origin of the app. If you need to access resources that live on a different web server, you need to either use a technique called JSONP or enable CORS headers on the remote resources.

Getting data from the server

The HttpRequest static method `getString()` is an easy way to get data from a web server. Use `then()` after `getString()` to specify the function that handles the string data:

```dart
import 'dart:html';
import 'dart:async';

// A JSON-formatted file in the same location as this page.
var uri = 'data.json';

main() {
  // Read a JSON file.
  HttpRequest.getString(uri).then(processString);
}

processString(String jsonText) {
  parseText(jsonText);
}
```

The function you specify (in the example, `processString()`) runs when the data at the specified URI is successfully retrieved. In this case, we are dynamically loading a JSON file. Information about the JSON API is in "Decoding and Encoding JSON" on page 96.

Add `.catchError()` after the call to `.then()` to specify an error handler:

---

53. *http://api.dartlang.org/dart_html/HttpRequest.html*

```
...
HttpRequest.getString(uri)
    .then(processString)
    .catchError(handleError);
...
handleError(error) {
  print('Uh oh, there was an error.');
  print(error.toString());
}
```

If you need access to the HttpRequest, not just the text data it retrieves, you can use the `request()` static method instead of `getString()`. Here's an example of reading XML data:

```
import 'dart:html';
import 'dart:async';

// An XML-formatted file in the same location as this page.
var xmlUri = 'data.xml';

main() {
  // Read an XML file.
  HttpRequest.request(xmlUri)
      .then(processRequest)
      .catchError(handleError);
}

processRequest(HttpRequest request) {
  var xmlDoc = request.responseXml;
  try {
    var license = xmlDoc.querySelector('license').text;
    print('License: $license');
  } catch(e) {
    print('$xmlUri doesn\'t have correct XML formatting.');
  }
}
...
```

You can also use the full API to handle more interesting cases. For example, you can set arbitrary headers.

The general flow for using the full API of HttpRequest is as follows:

1. Create the HttpRequest object.

2. Open the URL with either GET or POST.

3. Attach event handlers.

4. Send the request.

For example:

```
import 'dart:html';
...
var httpRequest = new HttpRequest()
    ..open('POST', dataUrl)
    ..onLoadEnd.listen((_) => requestComplete(httpRequest))
    ..send(encodedData);
```

Sending data to the server

HttpRequest can send data to the server using the HTTP method POST. For example, you might want to dynamically submit data to a form handler. Sending JSON data to a RESTful web service is another common example.

Submitting data to a form handler requires you to provide name-value pairs as URI-encoded strings. (Information about the URI class is in "URIs" on page 71.) You must also set the Content-type header to application/x-www-form-urlencode if you wish to send data to a form handler:

```
import 'dart:html';

String encodeMap(Map data) {
  return data.keys.map((k) {
    return '${Uri.encodeComponent(k)}=${Uri.encodeComponent(data[k])}';
  }).join('&');
}

loadEnd(HttpRequest request) {
  if (request.status != 200) {
    print('Uh oh, there was an error of ${request.status}');
  } else {
    print('Data has been posted');
  }
}

main() {
  var dataUrl = '/registrations/create';
  var data = {'dart': 'fun', 'editor': 'productive'};
  var encodedData = encodeMap(data);

  var httpRequest = new HttpRequest();
  httpRequest.open('POST', dataUrl);
  httpRequest.setRequestHeader('Content-type',
                        'application/x-www-form-urlencoded');
  httpRequest.onLoadEnd.listen((e) => loadEnd(httpRequest));
  httpRequest.send(encodedData);
}
```

Sending and Receiving Real-Time Data with WebSockets

A WebSocket allows your web app to exchange data with a server interactively—no polling necessary. A server creates the WebSocket and listens for requests on a URL that starts with **ws://**—for example, ws://127.0.0.1:1337/ws. The data transmitted over a WebSocket can be a string, a blob, or an ArrayBuffer.[54] Often, the data is a JSON-formatted string.

To use a WebSocket in your web app, first create a WebSocket[55] object, passing the WebSocket URL as an argument:

```
var ws = new WebSocket('ws://echo.websocket.org');
```

Sending data

To send string data on the WebSocket, use the send() method:

```
ws.send('Hello from Dart!');
```

Receiving data

To receive data on the WebSocket, register a listener for message events:

```
ws.onMessage.listen((MessageEvent e) {
  print('Received message: ${e.data}');
});
```

The message event handler receives a MessageEvent[56] object. This object's data field has the data from the server.

Handling WebSocket events

Your app can handle the following WebSocket events: open, close, error, and (as shown earlier) message. Here's an example of a method that creates a WebSocket object and registers handlers for open, close, error, and message events:

```
void initWebSocket([int retrySeconds = 2]) {
  var reconnectScheduled = false;

  print("Connecting to websocket");
  ws = new WebSocket('ws://echo.websocket.org');

  void scheduleReconnect() {
    if (!reconnectScheduled) {
      new Timer(new Duration(milliseconds: 1000 * retrySeconds),
              () => initWebSocket(retrySeconds * 2));
    }
    reconnectScheduled = true;
  }

  ws.onOpen.listen((e) {
```

---

54. *http://api.dartlang.org/html/ArrayBuffer.html*
55. *http://api.dartlang.org/html/WebSocket.html*
56. *http://api.dartlang.org/html/MessageEvent.html*

```
    print('Connected');
    ws.send('Hello from Dart!');
  });

  ws.onClose.listen((e) {
    print('Websocket closed, retrying in $retrySeconds seconds');
    scheduleReconnect();
  });

  ws.onError.listen((e) {
    print("Error connecting to ws");
    scheduleReconnect();
  });

  ws.onMessage.listen((MessageEvent e) {
    print('Received message: ${e.data}');
  });
}
```

For more information and examples of using WebSockets, see the Dart Code Samples[57].

More Information

This section barely scratched the surface of using the dart:html library. For more information, see the documentation for dart:html[58] and the code and explanations in the Dart Code Samples[59]. Dart has additional libraries for more specialized web APIs, such as web audio[60], IndexedDB[61], and WebGL[62].

dart:io—I/O for Command-Line Apps

The dart:io library[63] provides APIs to deal with files, directories, processes, sockets, WebSockets, and HTTP clients and servers. Only command-line apps can use dart:io —not web apps.

In general, the dart:io library implements and promotes an asynchronous API. Synchronous methods can easily block an application, making it difficult to scale. Therefore, most operations return results via Future or Stream objects, a pattern common with modern server platforms such as Node.js.

---

57. *http://www.dartlang.org/samples/*

58. *http://api.dartlang.org/dart_html.html*

59. *http://www.dartlang.org/samples/*

60. *http://api.dartlang.org/dart_web_audio.html*

61. *http://api.dartlang.org/dart_indexed_db.html*

62. *http://api.dartlang.org/dart_web_gl.html*

63. *http://api.dartlang.org/io.html*

The few synchronous methods in the dart:io library are clearly marked with a Sync suffix on the method name. We don't cover them here.

 Only command-line apps can import and use `dart:io`.

Files and Directories

The I/O library enables command-line apps to read and write files and browse directories. You have two choices for reading the contents of a file: all at once, or streaming. Reading a file all at once requires enough memory to store all the contents of the file. If the file is very large or you want to process it while reading it, you should use a Stream, as described in "Streaming file contents" on page 92.

Reading a file as text

When reading a text file encoded using UTF-8, you can read the entire file contents with `readAsString()`. When the individual lines are important, you can use `readAs Lines()`. In both cases, a Future object is returned that provides the contents of the file as one or more strings:

```
import 'dart:io';

main() {
  var config = new File('config.txt');

  // Put the whole file in a single string.
  config.readAsString().then((String contents) {
    print('The entire file is ${contents.length} characters long');
  });

  // Put each line of the file into its own string.
  config.readAsLines().then((List<String> lines) {
    print('The entire file is ${lines.length} lines long');
  });
}
```

Reading a file as binary

The following code reads an entire file as bytes into a list of ints. The call to `readAsBytes()` returns a Future, which provides the result when it's available:

```
import 'dart:io';

main() {
  var config = new File('config.txt');
```

```
    config.readAsBytes().then((List<int> contents) {
      print('The entire file is ${contents.length} bytes long');
    });
  }
```

Handling errors

To capture errors so they don't result in uncaught exceptions, you can register a catch
Error handler:

```
import 'dart:io';

main() {
  var config = new File('config.txt');
  config.readAsString().then((String contents) {
    print(contents);
  }).catchError((e) {
    print(e);
  });
}
```

Streaming file contents

Use a Stream to read a file, a little at a time. The listen() method specifies a handler
to be called when data is available. When the Stream is finished reading the file, the
onDone callback executes:

```
import 'dart:io';
import 'dart:convert';
import 'dart:async';

main() {
  var config = new File('config.txt');
  Stream<List<int>> inputStream = config.openRead();

  inputStream
    .transform(UTF8.decoder)
    .transform(new LineSplitter())
    .listen(
      (String line) {
        print('Got ${line.length} characters from stream');
      },
      onDone: () { print('file is now closed'); },
      onError: (e) { print(e.toString()); });
}
```

Writing file contents

You can use an IOSink[64] to write data to a file. Use the File `openWrite()` method to get an IOSink that you can write to. The default mode, `FileMode.WRITE`, completely overwrites existing data in the file:

```
var logFile = new File('log.txt');
var sink = logFile.openWrite();
sink.write('FILE ACCESSED ${new DateTime.now()}\n');
sink.close();
```

To add to the end of the file, use the optional `mode` parameter to specify `FileMode.APPEND`:

```
var sink = logFile.openWrite(mode: FileMode.APPEND);
```

To write binary data, use `add(List<int> data)`.

Listing files in a directory

Finding all files and subdirectories for a directory is an asynchronous operation. The `list()` method returns a Stream on which you can register handlers (using `listen()`) to be notified when a file or directory is encountered:

```
import 'dart:io';
import 'dart:async';

main() {
  var dir = new Directory('/tmp');
  var contentsStream = dir.list(recursive:true);
  contentsStream.listen(
    (FileSystemEntity f) {
      if (f is File) {
        print('Found file ${f.path}');
      } else if (f is Directory) {
        print('Found dir ${f.path}');
      }
    },
    onError: (e) { print(e.toString()); }
  );
}
```

Other common functionality

The File and Directory classes contain other functionality, including but not limited to:

- Creating a file or directory: `create()` in File and Directory
- Deleting a file or directory: `delete()` in File and Directory

---

64. *http://api.dartlang.org/dart_io/IOSink.html*

- Getting the length of a file: length() in File

- Getting random access to a file: open() in File

Refer to the API docs for File[65] and Directory[66] for a full list of methods.

HTTP Clients and Servers

The dart:io library provides classes that command-line apps can use for accessing HTTP resources, as well as running HTTP servers.

HTTP server

The HttpServer[67] class provides the low-level functionality for building web servers. You can match request handlers, set headers, stream data, and more.

The following sample web server can return only simple text information. This server listens on port 8888 and address 127.0.0.1 (localhost), responding to requests for the path /languages/dart. All other requests are handled by the default request handler, which returns a response code of 404 (not found):

```
import 'dart:io';

main() {
  dartHandler(HttpRequest request) {
    request.response.headers.contentType = new ContentType('text', 'plain');
    request.response.write('Dart is optionally typed');
    request.response.close();
  };

  HttpServer.bind('127.0.0.1', 8888).then((HttpServer server) {
    server.listen((request) {
      print('Got request for ${request.uri.path}');
      if (request.uri.path == '/languages/dart') {
        dartHandler(request);
      } else {
        request.response.write('Not found');
        request.response.close();
      }
    });
  });
}
```

---

65. *http://api.dartlang.org/io/File.html*

66. *http://api.dartlang.org/io/Directory.html*

67. *http://api.dartlang.org/dart_io/HttpServer.html*

For a more comprehensive HTTP server, see Chapter 5. It features the Dartiverse Search sample, which implements a web server using dart:io and packages such as http_server[68] and route[69].

HTTP client

The HttpClient[70] class helps you connect to HTTP resources from your Dart command-line or server-side application. You can set headers, use HTTP methods, and read and write data. The HttpClient class does not work in browser-based apps. When programming in the browser, use the HttpRequest class (page 86). Here's an example of using HttpClient:

```
import 'dart:io';
import 'dart:convert';

main() {
  var url = Uri.parse('http://127.0.0.1:8888/languages/dart');
  var httpClient = new HttpClient();
  httpClient.getUrl(url)
    .then((HttpClientRequest request) {
      print('have request');
      return request.close();
    })
    .then((HttpClientResponse response) {
      print('have response');
      response.transform(UTF8.decoder).toList().then((data) {
        var body = data.join('');
        print(body);
        httpClient.close();
      });
    });
}
```

More Information

Besides the APIs discussed in this section, the dart:io library also provides APIs for processes[71], sockets[72], and web sockets[73].

For more examples of using dart:io, see the Dart Code Samples[74].

---

68. *https://pub.dartlang.org/packages/http_server*

69. *http://pub.dartlang.org/packages/route*

70. *http://api.dartlang.org/dart_io/HttpClient.html*

71. *http://api.dartlang.org/io/Process.html*

72. *http://api.dartlang.org/io/Socket.html*

73. *http://api.dartlang.org/io/WebSocket.html*

74. *http://www.dartlang.org/samples/*

dart:convert—Decoding and Encoding JSON, UTF-8, and More

The dart:convert library[75] has converters for JSON and UTF-8, as well as support for creating additional converters. JSON is a simple text format for representing structured objects and collections. UTF-8 is a common variable-width encoding that can represent every character in the Unicode character set.

The dart:convert library works in both web apps and command-line apps. To use it, import dart:convert.

Decoding and Encoding JSON

Decode a JSON-encoded string into a Dart object with JSON.decode():

```
import 'dart:convert' show JSON;

main() {
  // NOTE: Be sure to use double quotes ("), not single quotes ('),
  // inside the JSON string. This string is JSON, not Dart.
  var jsonString = '''
  [
    {"score": 40},
    {"score": 80}
  ]
  ''';

  var scores = JSON.decode(jsonString);
  assert(scores is List);

  var firstScore = scores[0];
  assert(firstScore is Map);
  assert(firstScore['score'] == 40);
}
```

Encode a supported Dart object into a JSON-formatted string with JSON.encode():

```
import 'dart:convert' show JSON;

main() {
  var scores = [
    {'score': 40},
    {'score': 80},
    {'score': 100, 'overtime': true, 'special_guest': null}
  ];

  var jsonText = JSON.encode(scores);
  assert(jsonText == '[{"score":40},{"score":80},'
```

75. *http://api.dartlang.org/dart_convert.html*

```
                  '{"score":100,"overtime":true,'
                  '"special_guest":null}]');
  }
```

Only objects of type int, double, String, bool, null, List, or Map (with string keys) are directly encodable into JSON. List and Map objects are encoded recursively.

You have two options for encoding objects that aren't directly encodable. The first is to invoke encode() with a second argument: a function that returns an object that is directly encodable. Your second option is to omit the second argument, in which case the encoder calls the object's toJson() method.

Decoding and Encoding UTF-8 Characters

Use UTF8.decode() to decode UTF8-encoded bytes to a Dart string:

```
import 'dart:convert' show UTF8;

main() {
  var string = UTF8.decode([0xc3, 0x8e, 0xc3, 0xb1, 0xc5, 0xa3, 0xc3, 0xa9,
                            0x72, 0xc3, 0xb1, 0xc3, 0xa5, 0xc5, 0xa3, 0xc3,
                            0xae, 0xc3, 0xb6, 0xc3, 0xb1, 0xc3, 0xa5, 0xc4,
                            0xbc, 0xc3, 0xae, 0xc5, 0xbe, 0xc3, 0xa5, 0xc5,
                            0xa3, 0xc3, 0xae, 0xe1, 0xbb, 0x9d, 0xc3, 0xb1]);
  print(string); // 'Îñţérñåţîöñåļîžåţîờñ'
}
```

To convert a stream of UTF-8 characters into a Dart string, specify UTF8.decoder to the Stream transform() method:

```
inputStream
  .transform(UTF8.decoder)
  .transform(new LineSplitter())
  .listen(
    (String line) {
      print('Read ${line.length} bytes from stream');
    });
```

Use UTF8.encode() to encode a Dart string as a list of UTF8-encoded bytes:

```
import 'dart:convert' show UTF8;

main() {
  List<int> expected = [0xc3, 0x8e, 0xc3, 0xb1, 0xc5, 0xa3, 0xc3, 0xa9, 0x72,
                        0xc3, 0xb1, 0xc3, 0xa5, 0xc5, 0xa3, 0xc3, 0xae, 0xc3,
                        0xb6, 0xc3, 0xb1, 0xc3, 0xa5, 0xc4, 0xbc, 0xc3, 0xae,
                        0xc5, 0xbe, 0xc3, 0xa5, 0xc5, 0xa3, 0xc3, 0xae, 0xe1,
                        0xbb, 0x9d, 0xc3, 0xb1];

  List<int> encoded = UTF8.encode('Îñţérñåţîöñåļîžåţîờñ');

  assert(() {
    if (encoded.length != expected.length) return false;
```

```
   for (int i = 0; i < encoded.length; i++) {
     if (encoded[i] != expected[i]) return false;
   }
   return true;
 });
}
```

Other Functionality

The dart:convert library also has converters for ASCII and ISO-8859-1 (Latin1). For details, see the API docs for the dart:convert library[76].

dart:mirrors—Reflection

The dart:mirrors library provides basic reflection abilities to Dart. Use mirrors to query the structure of your program and to dynamically invoke functions or methods at runtime.

The dart:mirrors library works in both web apps and command-line apps. To use it, import dart:mirrors.

 Using dart:mirrors can cause dart2js to generate very large JavaScript files.

The current workaround is to add a @MirrorsUsed annotation before the import of dart:mirrors. For details, see the MirrorsUsed[77] API documentation. This workaround is very likely to change, as the dart:mirrors library is still under development.

Symbols

The mirror system represents the names of Dart declarations (classes, fields, and so on) by instances of the class Symbol[78]. Symbols work even in code where names have changed due to minification.

When you know the name of the symbol ahead of time, use a symbol literal. This way, repeated uses of the same symbol can use the same canonicalized instance. If the name of the symbol is determined dynamically at runtime, use the Symbol constructor:

```
import 'dart:mirrors';

// If the symbol name is known at compile time.
const className = #MyClass;
```

---

76. *http://api.dartlang.org/dart_convert.html*
77. *http://api.dartlang.org/dart_mirrors/MirrorsUsed.html*
78. *http://api.dartlang.org/dart_core/Symbol.html*

```
// If the symbol name is dynamically determined.
var userInput = askUserForNameOfFunction();
var functionName = new Symbol(userInput);
```

During minification, a compiler might replace a symbol name with a different (often smaller) name. To convert from a symbol back to a string, use `MirrorSystem.get Name()`. This function returns the correct name, even if the code was minified:

```
import 'dart:mirrors';

const className = #MyClass;
assert('MyClass' == MirrorSystem.getName(className));
```

Introspection

Use mirrors to introspect the running program's structure. You can inspect classes, libraries, instances, and more.

The examples in this section use the following Person class:

```
class Person {
  String firstName;
  String lastName;
  int age;

  Person(this.firstName, this.lastName, this.age);

  String get fullName => '$firstName $lastName';

  void greet(String other) {
    print('Hello there, $other!');
  }
}
```

To begin, you need to *reflect* on a class or object to get its *mirror*.

Class Mirrors

Reflect on a Type to get its ClassMirror:

```
ClassMirror mirror = reflectClass(Person);

assert('Person' == MirrorSystem.getName(mirror.simpleName));
```

You can also call `runtimeType` to get a Type from an instance:

```
var person = new Person('Bob', 'Smith', 33);
ClassMirror mirror = reflectClass(person.runtimeType);

assert('Person' == MirrorSystem.getName(mirror.simpleName));
```

Once you have a ClassMirror, you can get a class's constructors, fields, and more. Here is an example of listing the constructors of a class:

```
showConstructors(ClassMirror mirror) {
  var constructors = mirror.declarations.values
      .where((m) => m is MethodMirror && m.isConstructor);

  constructors.forEach((m) {
    print('The constructor ${m.simpleName} has '
          '${m.parameters.length} parameters.');
  });
}
```

Here is an example of listing all of the fields declared by a class:

```
showFields(ClassMirror mirror) {
  var fields = mirror.declarations.values.where((m) => m is VariableMirror);

  fields.forEach((VariableMirror m) {
    var finalStatus = m.isFinal ? 'final' : 'not final';
    var privateStatus = m.isPrivate ? 'private' : 'not private';
    var typeAnnotation = m.type.simpleName;

    print('The field ${m.simpleName} is $privateStatus and $finalStatus '
          'and is annotated as $typeAnnotation.');
  });
}
```

For a full list of methods, consult the API docs for ClassMirror[79].

InstanceMirrors

Reflect on an object to get an InstanceMirror:

```
var p = new Person('Bob', 'Smith', 42);
InstanceMirror mirror = reflect(p);
```

If you have an InstanceMirror and you want to get the object that it reflects, use `reflectee`:

```
var person = mirror.reflectee;
assert(identical(p, person));
```

Invocation

Once you have an InstanceMirror, you can invoke methods and call getters and setters. For a full list of methods, consult the API docs for InstanceMirror[80].

---

79. *http://api.dartlang.org/dart_mirrors/ClassMirror.html*

80. *http://api.dartlang.org/dart_mirrors/InstanceMirror.html*

Invoke methods

Use InstanceMirror's `invoke()` method to invoke a method on an object. The first parameter specifies the method to be invoked, and the second is a list of positional arguments to the method. An optional third parameter lets you specify named arguments:

```
var p = new Person('Bob', 'Smith', 42);
InstanceMirror mirror = reflect(p);

mirror.invoke(#greet, ['Shailen']);
```

Invoke getters and setters

Use InstanceMirror's `getField()` and `setField()` methods to get and set properties of an object:

```
var p = new Person('Bob', 'Smith', 42);
InstanceMirror mirror = reflect(p);

// Get the value of a property.
var fullName = mirror.getField(#fullName).reflectee;
assert(fullName == 'Bob Smith');

// Set the value of a property.
mirror.setField(#firstName, 'Mary');
assert(p.firstName == 'Mary');
```

More Information

The article Reflection in Dart with Mirrors[81] has more information and examples. Also see the API docs for dart:mirror[82], especially MirrorsUsed[83], ClassMirror[84], and InstanceMirror.[85]

Summary

This chapter introduced you to the most commonly used functionality in many of Dart's built-in libraries. It didn't cover all the built-in libraries, however. Others that you might want to look into include dart:collection[86], dart:isolate[87], dart:js[88], and dart:typed_data.

---

81. *https://www.dartlang.org/articles/reflection-with-mirrors/*

82. *http://api.dartlang.org/dart_mirrors.html*

83. *http://api.dartlang.org/dart_mirrors/MirrorsUsed.html*

84. *http://api.dartlang.org/dart_mirrors/ClassMirror.html*

85. *http://api.dartlang.org/dart_mirrors/InstanceMirror.html*

86. *http://api.dartlang.org/dart_collection.html*

87. *http://api.dartlang.org/dart_isolate.html*

88. *http://api.dartlang.org/dart_js.html*

[89] You can get yet more libraries by using the pub tool, discussed in the next chapter. The args[90], logging[91], polymer[92], and unittest[93] libraries are just a sampling of what you can install using pub.

89. *http://api.dartlang.org/dart_typed_data.html*

90. *http://pub.dartlang.org/packages/args*

91. *http://api.dartlang.org/logging.html*

92. *http://pub.dartlang.org/packages/polymer*

93. *http://api.dartlang.org/unittest.html*

CHAPTER 4

Tools

Dart provides several tools to help you write and deploy your web and command-line apps. These tools include:

pub: The Dart package manager (page 104)
Download and install packages of libraries.

Dart Editor (page 105)
Edit, run, and debug web and command-line apps.

Dartium: Chromium with the Dart VM (page 113)
Run Dart web apps. This is a special build of Chromium (the project behind Google Chrome).

dart2js: The Dart-to-JavaScript compiler (page 116)
Convert your web app to JavaScript, so it can run in non-Dartium browsers.

dart: The standalone Dart VM (page 120)
Run your command-line apps—server-side scripts, programs, servers, and any other apps that don't run in a browser.

dartanalyzer: The Static Analyzer (page 121)
Analyze your Dart source from the command line.

All of these tools are in the Dart Editor bundle, since the editor uses them. You can also download Dartium separately, and you can download an SDK that includes pub, dart2js, dart, dartanalyzer, and more. See the Tools page[1] for links and details.

The tools are in the `dart-sdk/bin` directory of your Dart installation directory. If you intend to use tools such as pub, dart2js, and dart from the command line, add the `bin` directory to your path.

---

1. *http://www.dartlang.org/tools/*

pub: The Dart Package Manager

You can use the *pub* tool to manage Dart packages. A Dart package is simply a directory containing any number of Dart libraries and a list of the library dependencies. A package can also contain resources for its libraries, such as documentation, tests, and images. If your app uses one or more packages, then your app itself must be a package.

 Dart Editor offers support for using pub, including creating, installing, updating, and publishing packages.

A package can live anywhere. For example, some packages are on GitHub. The Dart team publishes packages at pub.dartlang.org, and we hope you will, too.

To use a library that's in a Dart package, you need to do the following:

1. Create a pubspec (a file that lists package dependencies and includes other metadata, such as a name for your package).
2. Use pub to get your package's dependencies.
3. Import the library.

Creating a Pubspec

To use a package, your application must define a pubspec that lists dependencies and their download locations. The pubspec is a file named `pubspec.yaml`, and it must be in the top directory of your application.

Here is an example of a pubspec that specifies the locations of two packages. First, it points to the js package that's hosted on pub.dartlang.org, and then it points to the intl package in the Dart SDK:

```
name: my_app
dependencies:
  js: any
  intl: any
```

For details, see the pubspec documentation[2] and the documentation for the packages you're interested in using.

---

2. *http://pub.dartlang.org/doc/pubspec.html*

Installing Packages

Once you have a pubspec, you can run `pub get` from the top directory of your application:

```
cd path/to/my_app
pub get
```

This command determines which packages your app depends on, and puts them in a central cache. For git dependencies, pub clones the git repository. For hosted dependencies, pub downloads the package from pub.dartlang.org. Transitive dependencies are included, too. For example, if the js package depends on the unittest package, the pub tool grabs both the js package and the unittest package.

Finally, pub creates a `packages` directory (under your app's top directory) that has links to the packages that your app depends on.

Importing Libraries from Packages

To import libraries found in packages, use the `package:` prefix:

```
import 'package:js/js.dart' as js;
import 'package:intl/intl.dart';
```

The Dart runtime takes everything after `package:` and looks it up within the `packages` directory for your app.

More Information

Pub has support for building web apps. If your web app's directory structure follows pub's package layout conventions,[3] you can use the pub development server (`pub serve`) to continuously build and serve the app's assets. Once you're ready to deploy the web app, use `pub build` to generate the final files.

For more information about pub, see the pub documentation.[4]

Dart Editor

We already introduced Dart Editor in "Up and Running" on page 5. Here are some more tips on using Dart Editor, with information such as specifying a browser (page 111) and compiling to JavaScript (page 112). If you run into a problem, see Troubleshooting Dart

---

3. *http://bit.ly/1h6jPN0*
4. *http://pub.dartlang.org/doc*

Editor[5]. Dart Editor is updated frequently, so it probably looks different from what you see here. For the latest information, see the Dart Editor documentation.[6]

Viewing Samples

The Welcome page of Dart Editor (Figure 1-2) displays a few samples. To open a sample and look at its source code, click the sample's image.

If you don't see the Welcome page, you probably closed it. Get it back with **Tools→Welcome Page**.

Managing the Files View

The Files view shows the files that implement the libraries included in Dart, installed packages, as well as all the apps that you create or open.

Adding apps

Here's how to open an app, which makes it appear in your Files view:

1. Go to the **File** menu, and choose **Open Existing Folder...**. Or use the keyboard shortcut (**Ctrl+O** or, on Mac, **Command-O**).
2. Browse to the directory that contains the app's files.
3. Click **Open**.

The directory and all its files appear in the Files view.

Removing apps

You can remove an app from the Files view, either with or without deleting its files.

Right-click (or Control-click) the directory and choose **Delete**. If you want to delete the app's files permanently, then in the dialog that comes up, choose **Delete project contents on disk**.

Creating Apps

It's easy to create a simple web or command-line app from scratch:

1. Click the New Application button ⊞ (at the upper-left of Dart Editor). Alternatively, choose **File→New Application** from the Dart Editor menu. A dialog appears.

---

5. *http://bit.ly/1h6jV7i*
6. *http://www.dartlang.org/editor*

2. Type in a name for your application—for example, `hello_web`. If you don't like the default parent directory, type in a new location or browse to choose the location.

3. Unless you really don't want files to be automatically created for you, make sure **Generate sample content** is selected.

4. Select the kind of application you're writing, such as command line, web, or web using Polymer.dart[7].

5. Click **Finish** to create a directory with initial files for the app.

   A default Dart file appears in the Edit view, and its directory appears in the Files view. Your Dart Editor window should look something like Figure 4-1.

Figure 4-1. A new app, pre-filled with basic, runnable code

Editing Apps

Dart Editor provides the basic editing functionality you'd expect, plus features such as Dart code completion, API browsing, support for refactoring, and the ability to search multiple files.

Using autocomplete

Autocomplete suggestions look something like Figure 4-2. They appear when you either:

- Type a class or variable name, and then type a period.

---

7. *http://www.dartlang.org/polymer-dart/*

For example, type **document.** or **DateTime.** and pause a moment. Once the suggestions appear, continue typing to pare down the list.

- Press **Ctrl+Space**.

  For example, type **Dat**, then Ctrl+Space to see a list of classes that start with "Dat".

When the suggestions come up, you can click, type, or use the arrow keys to select the one you want. Press Enter or Return to choose a suggestion, or Esc to dismiss the panel.

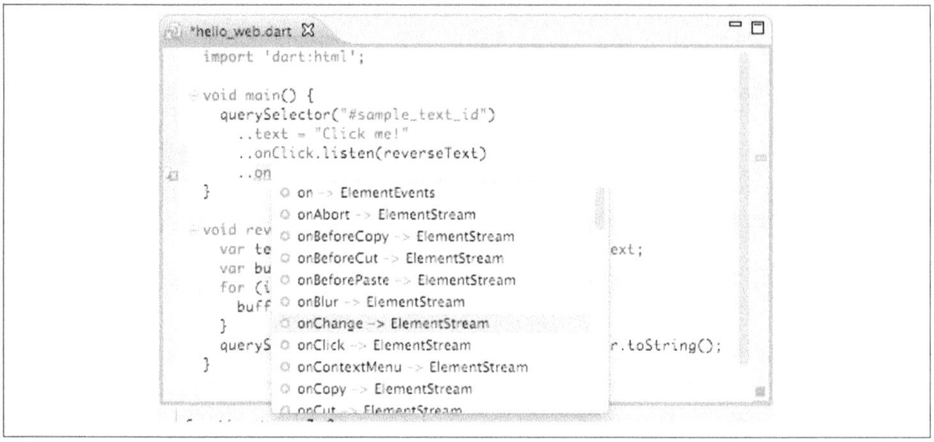

Figure 4-2. Autocomplete suggestions

Browsing APIs

With Dart Editor you can easily find where APIs are declared. You can also outline the contents of a Dart file.

Finding out more about an API. To get more information about an API item—variable, method, type, library, and so on—hover the mouse over the item in the Edit view. Dart Editor displays a popup that provides more information about that item.

To go to the declaration of an API item, either within the same .dart file or in another file:

1. In the Edit view of a Dart file, click on an API item. Dart Editor highlights the item and all other occurrences of the item.

2. Right-click and choose **Open Declaration** from the menu.

   The editor displays the file that declares the item. For example, if you open the declaration for querySelector, the file that declares the `querySelector()` function appears.

Outlining a file's contents. Press **Alt+O** (**Option-O** on Mac) or right-click and choose **Outline File**.

A panel comes up displaying the classes, methods, and fields declared in the current Dart file. For example, the outline for the Sunflower sample's `sunflower.dart` file looks something like Figure 4-3.

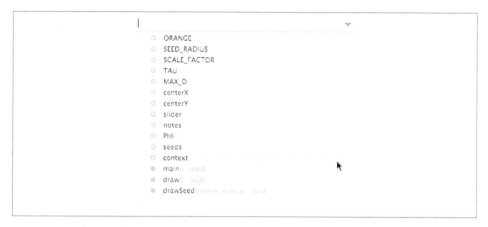

Figure 4-3. The Outline panel for the Sunflower sample

You can reduce the size of the list by typing one or more characters. For example, if you type **c**, only the **center** and **context** variables appear.

If you choose an item from the list—for example, **centerX**—the editor scrolls to its declaration.

Alternatively, add a more permanent outline view by choosing **Tools→Outline**.

Refactoring

To change the name of an item throughout your code, put the cursor within (or double-click) the item's name in the Edit view, and right-click and choose **Rename....**

You can rename almost anything—local variables, function parameters, fields, methods, types, top-level functions, library prefixes, top-level compilation units, and more. An example of renaming a top-level compilation unit is changing the name of a file that's sourced by a library.

Searching

The search field at the upper right of the Dart Editor window is an easy way to go directly to:

- Types
- Files
- Text inside of files

The scope of a text search is every file in your Files view. Results for text searches come up in a Search view. Within that view, double-click a file to see it in the Edit view. All occurrences of the search string in the Edit view are highlighted.

Running Apps

To run any Dart app, click Dart Editor's Run button ⊙ while a file in that app is selected. If you're working on a web app, Dart Editor brings up a browser window that displays the app's HTML page, with the app's code running inside it.

When you run a web application using Dart Editor, by default the app uses the copy of Dartium that's included in the Dart Editor download, with the Dart code executing directly in the browser. If your launch configuration specifies a browser, then Dart Editor uses dart2js (page 116) to compile the Dart code to JavaScript that executes in the browser.

Specifying launch configurations

Use **Run→Manage Launches** to specify as many launch configurations as you like.

For web apps, you can specify the following:

- HTML file or URL to open
- Arguments to pass to the browser; for example, `--allow-file-access-from-files`
- Checked mode (Dartium only)
- Enable experimental features (Dartium only)
- Whether to show the browser's stdout and stderr output (Dartium only; useful for diagnosing Dartium crashes)

For example, a web app might have a launch configuration for Dartium and several more configurations corresponding to additional browsers you want to test.

You can specify the following for command-line apps:

- .dart file to execute
- Working directory
- Arguments to pass to the app
- Checked mode

Running in production mode

By default, apps run in checked mode. To run in production mode instead, disable checked mode in your app's launch configuration:

1. Run your app at least once, so that it has a launch configuration.
2. Choose **Run→Manage Launches**, or click the little arrow to the right of the Run button ⊙ and choose **Manage Launches**.
3. In the Manage Launches dialog, find a launch configuration for your app. Click it if it isn't already selected.
4. Unselect **Run in checked mode** (see Figure 4-4).

Figure 4-4. To run in production mode, unselect checked mode

5. Click **Apply** to save your change, or **Run** to save it and run your app.

For details about checked mode and production mode, see "Runtime Modes" on page 14.

Specifying a browser for JavaScript launches

To specify the browser in which to run the JavaScript version of your web apps:

1. Choose **Dart Editor→Preferences**.
2. Click **Run and Debug**.
3. Unless you want to use the default system browser, deselect **Use default system browser** and specify the location of the browser you want to use. For example, */Applications/Firefox.app*.
4. Click **OK** to save your changes.

Now whenever you run an app as JavaScript, Dart Editor invokes your browser of choice.

Alternatively, you can run your app as JavaScript using the default browser setting and then copy and paste the URL into a different browser.

Debugging Apps

You can debug both command-line and web apps with Dart Editor. Here are some tips:

* Set breakpoints by double-clicking in the left margin of the Edit view.

- Use the Debugger view to view your app's state and control its execution. By default, the Debugger view is to the right of the Edit view and appears when you first hit a breakpoint (Figure 4-5).

- To see the value of a variable, mouse over it, look in the Debugger view, or use an Expression ⚙.

- To debug web apps, use Dart Editor with Dartium. While you're debugging, Dart Editor takes the place of the Dartium console. For example, Dart Editor displays the output of `print()` statements.

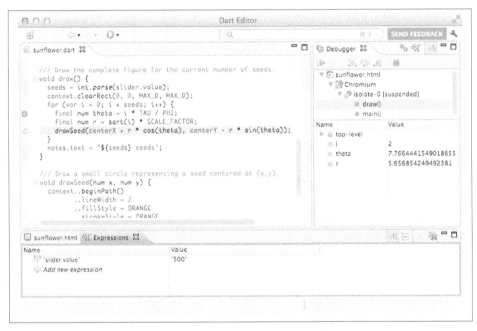

Figure 4-5. Using Dart Editor to debug the Sunflower sample app

Compiling to JavaScript

You might not need to do anything to compile your code to JavaScript. When you run an app using a launch configuration that specifies a browser (page 111), Dart Editor automatically compiles the app to JavaScript before executing it in the browser.

However, you can also compile Dart code to JavaScript without running the app. Just choose **Tools→Generate JavaScript**. Another option is using dart2js from the command line (see "dart2js: The Dart-to-JavaScript Compiler" on page 116).

Other Features

Dart Editor has many additional features, including customization and keyboard alternatives.

Customizing Dart Editor

You can customize the editor's font, margins, key bindings, and more using the Preferences dialog. To bring up the dialog, choose **Tools→Preferences** (on Mac: **Dart Editor→Preferences**).

You can also customize which views you see in Dart Editor, as well as their size and position. To add views, use the **Tools** menu. To remove a view, click its **X**. To move a view, drag its tab to a different position, either within or outside of the Dart Editor window. To resize a view, drag its edges.

Keyboard alternatives

To get a list of all keyboard alternatives, choose **Help→Key Assist** (Figure 4-6).

Backward History	⌘[
Close	⌘W
Close All	⇧⌘W
Content Assist	^Space
Copy	⌘C
Copy Lines	⌥⌘↓
Cut	⌘X
Delete	⌦
Delete Line	⌘D
Delete Next Word	⌥⌦
Delete Previous Word	⌥⌫
Delete to End of Line	⇧⌘⌦
Duplicate Lines	⌥⌘↑
Extract Local Variable	⌥⌘L
Extract Method	⌥⌘M
Find Callers	^⌥H
Find Next	⌘K
Find Previous	⇧⌘K

Press '⇧⌘L' to open the preference page.

Figure 4-6. Help→Key Assist

Dartium: Chromium with the Dart VM

This section tells you how to get and use Dartium, a Chromium-based browser that includes the Dart VM. This browser can execute Dart web apps directly, so you don't have to compile your code to JavaScript until you're ready to test on other browsers.

This browser is a technical preview, and it might have security and stability issues. **Do not use Dartium as your primary browser, and do not distribute Dartium to users!**

Downloading and Installing the Browser

If you have an up-to-date version of Dart Editor, you already have Dartium.

If you don't have Dart Editor or want a different version of Dartium, you can get it separately from the Dartium page[8].

You don't usually need to do anything special to install Dartium: just unarchive the ZIP file. If you want Dart Editor to launch a particular copy of Dartium, then put that copy in the same directory as the dart-sdk directory of your Dart installation directory (see "Step 1: Download and Install the Software" on page 5), replacing the original copy of Chromium.

The Dartium binary expires after a couple of months. When that happens, you'll need to download a new binary unless you're using the Dartium binary that comes with Dart Editor. (Dart Editor automatically updates its Dartium binary.)

Launching the Browser

To launch Dartium, navigate to its directory in your finder, and double-click the Chromium executable file. Or use Dart Editor as described in "Running Apps" on page 110 or the command line as described in "Launching from the Command Line" on page 115.

If you already use Chromium: If another version of Chromium is open, then you could have a profile conflict. To avoid this, you can open Dartium or Chromium from the command line with the --user-data-dir flag.[9]

Filing Bugs

If you find a bug in Dartium, create an issue in the Dart project and use the Dartium bug template[10].

Linking to Dart Source

Use a script tag with a type application/dart to link to your Dart source file. For example:

---

8. *http://www.dartlang.org/downloads.html*
9. *http://bit.ly/1kX4S51*
10. *http://bit.ly/WO0U32*

```html
<!DOCTYPE html>
<html>
  <body>
    <script type="application/dart" src="app.dart"></script>

    <!-- Support for non-Dart browsers. -->
    <script src="packages/browser/dart.js"></script>
  </body>
</html>
```

 Dart Editor automatically adds both the `application/dart` script tag and the `dart.js` script tag into the project's main HTML file.

For more information on linking to source code, see the article "Embedding Dart in HTML[11]."

Detecting Dart Support

You can check whether a browser supports Dart with this JavaScript code:

```javascript
// In JavaScript code:
if (navigator.userAgent.indexOf('(Dart)') == -1) {
  // No native Dart support...
  window.addEventListener("DOMContentLoaded", function (e) {
    // ...Fall back to compiled JS...
  }
}, false);
}
```

Launching from the Command Line

Because Dartium is based on Chromium, all Chromium flags[12] should work. In some cases, you might want to specify Dart-specific flags so that you can tweak the embedded Dart VM's behavior. For example, while developing your web app, you might want the VM to verify type annotations and check assertions. To achieve that, you can enable checked mode (the VM's `--checked` flag).

On Linux, you can specify flags by starting Dartium as follows:

```
DART_FLAGS='--checked' path/chrome
```

On Mac:

---

11. *http://bit.ly/1kX4X8M*
12. *http://bit.ly/1bLGsJ0*

```
DART_FLAGS='--checked'                  \
    path/Chromium.app/Contents/MacOS/Chromium
```

Or (also on Mac):

```
DART_FLAGS='--checked'                  \
    open path/Chromium.app
```

 You can see the command-line flags and executable path of any Chromium-based browser by going to chrome://version.

dart2js: The Dart-to-JavaScript Compiler

Use the *dart2js* tool to compile Dart code to JavaScript. Dart Editor (page 112) uses dart2js behind the scenes whenever Dart Editor compiles to JavaScript. The pub tool's serve and build options also use dart2js.

The dart2js tool provides hints for improving your Dart code and removing unused code. You can get these hints for all kinds of code—even command-line apps. Also see dartanalyzer, which performs a similar analysis but, as of 1.0, has a different implementation.

This section tells you how to use dart2js on the command line. It also give tips on debugging the JavaScript that dart2js generates.

Basic Usage

Here's an example of compiling a Dart file to JavaScript:

```
dart2js --out=test.js test.dart
```

This command produces a file that contains the JavaScript equivalent of your Dart code. It also produces a source map, which can help you debug the JavaScript version of the app more easily.

Options

Common command-line options for dart2js include:

-o *<file>* or --out=*<file>*
Generate the output into *<file>*; if not specified, the output goes in a file named out.js

-c *or* --checked
Insert runtime type checks, and enable assertions (checked mode)

`-m` *or* `--minify`
> Generate minified output

`-h` *or* `--help`
> Display help (use `-vh` for information about all options)

Some other handy options include:

`-p<path>` *or* `--package-root=<path>`
> Specify where to find "package:" imports

`-D<flag>=<value>`
> Define an environment variable

`--version`
> Display version information for dart2js

The following options help you control the output of dart2js:

`--suppress-warnings`
> Don't display warnings

`--suppress-hints`
> Don't display hints

`--terse`
> Emit diagnostics, but don't suggest how to get rid of the diagnosed problems

`-v` *or* `--verbose`
> Display lots of information

The following options control the analysis that dart2js performs on Dart code:

`--analyze-all`
> Analyze even the code that isn't reachable from `main()`; useful for finding errors in
> libraries, but using it can result in bigger and slower output

`--analyze-only`
> Analyze the code, but don't generate code

`--analyze-signatures-only`
> Similar to `--analyze-only`, but skip analysis of method bodies and field initializers

`--categories=Server`
> Use with `--analyze-only` to analyze a command-line app; default category is `Cli`
> `ent`, which tells dart2js to expect a web app

Helping dart2js Generate Better Code

You can do a couple of things to improve the code that dart2js generates:

- Write your code in a way that makes type inference easier.
- Once you're ready to deploy your app, use the dart2js `--minify` option to reduce code size.

 Don't worry about the size of your app's included libraries. The dart2js tool performs tree shaking to omit unused classes, functions, methods, and so on. Just import the libraries you need, and let dart2js get rid of what you don't need.

Follow these practices to help dart2js do better type inference, so it can generate smaller and faster JavaScript code:

- Avoid using the dart:mirrors library, directly or indirectly. If you must use it, provide `@MirrorsUsed` annotations.
- Don't use `Function.apply()`.
- Don't override `noSuchMethod()`.
- Avoid setting variables to null.
- Be consistent with the types of arguments you pass into each function or method.

Debugging

This section gives tips for debugging dart2js-produced code in Chrome, Firefox, and Safari. Debugging the JavaScript produced by dart2js is easiest in browsers such as Chrome that support source maps.

Whichever browser you use, you should enable pausing on at least uncaught exceptions, and perhaps on all exceptions. For frameworks such as dart:isolate and dart:async that wrap user code in try-catch, we recommend pausing on all exceptions.

Chrome

To debug in Chrome:

1. Open the Developer Tools window, as described in the Chrome DevTools documentation[13].
2. Turn on source maps, as described in the video SourceMaps in Chrome[14].

---

13. *http://bit.ly/1blC6aZ*
14. *http://bit.ly/YugIUY*

3. Enable debugging, either on all exceptions or only on uncaught exceptions, as described in Pause on JavaScript exceptions[15].

4. Reload your application.

Firefox

Firefox doesn't yet support source maps (see bug #771597[16]). To debug in Firefox:

1. Enable the Developer Toolbar, as described in Kevin Dangoor's blog post, "New Firefox Command Line Helps You Develop Faster[17]."

2. Click the **Debugger** button at the bottom of the browser, and enable **Pause on exceptions** (see Figure 4-7).

3. Reload your application.

Figure 4-7. Firefox's Developer Toolbar

Safari

To debug in Safari:

1. Turn on the Develop menu, as described in the Safari Web Inspector Guide[18].

2. Enable breaks, either on all exceptions or only on uncaught exceptions. See Figure 4-2 on the Safari Debugging[19] page.

3. Reload your application.

---

15. *http://bit.ly/1fdBFR8*
16. *http://mzl.la/1fyYb1A*
17. *http://mzl.la/1jH0gwy*
18. *http://bit.ly/1fdBKEf*
19. *http://bit.ly/MzWaeF*

dart: The Standalone VM

You can use the *dart* tool (`bin/dart`) to run Dart command-line apps such as server-side scripts, programs, and servers. During development, you also have the option to run command-line apps using Dart Editor (page 110).

Basic Usage

Here's an example of running a Dart file on the command line:

```
dart test.dart
```

Options

Common command-line options for dart include:

`-c` *or* `--checked`
> Enable *both* assertions and type checks (checked mode).

`-p<path>` or `-package-root=<path>`
> Specify where to find imported libraries.

`--version`
> Display VM version information.

`-h` *or* `--help`
> Display help. (Add `-v` for information about all options.)

You can also generate snapshots:

`--snapshot=<filename>`
> Generate a snapshot in the specified file. For information on generating and running snapshots, see the article Snapshots in Dart[20].

Enabling Checked Mode

Dart programs run in one of two modes: checked or production. By default, the Dart VM runs in production mode. We recommend that you enable checked mode for development and testing.

In checked mode, assignments are dynamically checked, and certain violations of the type system raise exceptions at runtime. In production mode, static type annotations have no effect.

---

20. *http://bit.ly/1fyYnxW*

Assert statements are also enabled in checked mode. An assert statement (page 36) checks a boolean condition, raising an exception if the condition is false. Assertions do not run in production mode.

You can run the VM in checked mode with the `--checked` command-line flag:

```
dart --checked test.dart
```

dartanalyzer: The Static Analyzer

You can use the *dartanalyzer* tool (`bin/dartanalyzer`) to statically analyze your code at the command line, checking for errors and warnings that are specified in the Dart Language Specification[21].

 Dart Editor performs the same analysis that dartanalyzer does. A previous static analyzer, called *dart_analyzer*, is no longer supported.

Basic Usage

Here's an example of testing a Dart file:

```
dartanalyzer --package-root=code/packages test.dart
```

As Table 4-1 shows, the exit code of dartanalyzer tells you whether the code passed analysis.

Table 4-1. Exit codes for dartanalyzer

Exit code	Description
0	No issues found
1	Warnings found (but no errors)
2	Errors found

Options

You can use the following command-line options with dartanalyzer:

`--dart-sdk=<path>`
Specify the directory that contains the Dart SDK

`-p<path>` *or* `--package-root=<path>`
Specify the directory to search for any libraries that are imported using `package:`

---

21. *http://www.dartlang.org/docs/spec/*

`--package-warnings`
> Show warnings not only for code in the specified .dart file and others in its library, but also for libraries imported with `package:`

`--format=machine`
> Produce output in a format suitable for parsing

`--no-hints`
> Don't show hints for improving the code

`--version`
> Show the analyzer version

`-h` *or* `--help`
> Show all the command-line options

Summary

This chapter covered the most commonly used Dart tools. All of them are available in the Dart Editor download, but you can also download Dartium or the SDK separately.

CHAPTER 5

Walkthrough: Dartiverse Search

This chapter points out some of the useful and fun features of the Dart language and libraries that are used in Dartiverse Search, a client-server app. As Figure 5-1 shows, Dartiverse Search looks for a user-entered string in GitHub and StackOverflow. The app is asynchronous, adding results as they're found, so the UI is always responsive.

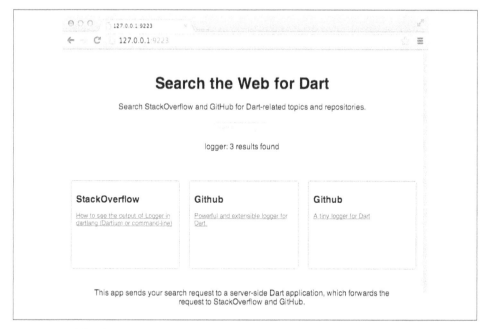

Figure 5-1. The client app UI

How to Run Dartiverse Search

You can use Dart Editor to get and run Dartiverse Search:

1. In Dart Editor, go to the Welcome page. (If you don't see it, choose **Tools→Welcome Page**.)
2. In the demo section, click **Dartiverse Search** to create a copy of the dartiverse_search package.[1]
3. Use **Tools→Pub Build** to build the package.
4. Select bin/server.dart and click the **Run** button. You should see a message that the search server is running at http://127.0.0.1:9223/.
5. Click that URL or enter it into any modern browser. The search client UI should appear in your default browser.

How Dartiverse Search Works

The search server is an HTTP server that provides a WebSocket interface. The search client uses that WebSocket interface as a bi-directional communication channel with the server. The client sends search requests to the server over the WebSocket, and the server replies with any results and then a final, "search done" message.

The server starts things off by binding to localhost, port 9223, and listening for requests to the WebSocket: ws://127.0.0.1:9223/ws. Search clients can connect using that URL.

The real communication between client and server happens when the user enters a search string. As Figure 5-2 shows, the client sends a JSON-encoded search request to the server. The server extracts the search string from the request and sends it to a series of search engines. Each search engine searches a specific site—for example, GitHub—using whatever API that site supports. Whenever a search engine finds a result, the server forwards that result to the client, again using a JSON-encoded message.

The search server implements an HTTP server that both provides content for the client UI and listens for WebSocket requests.

The client code is split between HTML (page structure), CSS (page look), and JavaScript (logic and behavior). That's typical of web clients.

The twist is that this client's JavaScript code is produced from Dart code, thanks to the dart2js compiler. Any modern browser can run this JavaScript code.

---

1. If you aren't using Dart Editor, you can find the Dartiverse Search source code in the Dart project under *samples/dartiverse_search*.

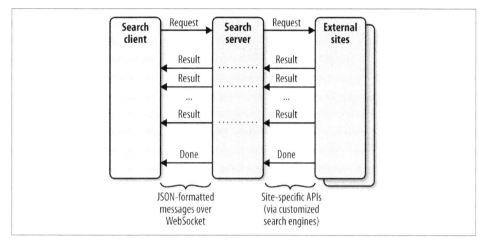

Figure 5-2. Communication in Dartiverse Search

The Client's HTML Code

The client's UI is simple. It has a search field, implemented as an <input> element named "q". It displays output in two <div>s named "status" and "results".

```
<!-- In web/index.html: -->

<input type="search" placeholder="Search" value="" id="q" disabled />
<div id="status"></div>
...
<div id="results"></div>
```

A couple of <script> tags tell the browser to execute the client's Dart or JavaScript code:

```
<script type="application/dart" src="client.dart"></script>
<script src="packages/browser/dart.js"></script>
```

The first line works in browsers that have an embedded Dart VM and so can execute Dart code; currently, only Dartium qualifies.

The second line is important for every other browser. It executes dart.js, which is a standard script that converts all Dart <script> tags to use foo.dart.js instead of foo.dart, with the assumption that foo.dart.js is a JavaScript version of foo.dart. For non-Dartium browsers, dart.js changes the first <script> tag to the following:

```
<script src="client.dart.js"></script>
```

You can get dart.js with the browser package from pub. See "dart2js: The Dart-to-JavaScript Compiler" on page 116 for more information about compiling Dart code into its JavaScript equivalent.

The Client's Dart Code

Dart code (`web/client.dart`) provides the client's logic, using the DOM to interact with UI elements. For example, the client's Dart code uses the DOM to find the div where the client displays messages.

Finding DOM Elements

The client app uses dart:html's top-level `querySelector()` function to get the client's UI elements from the DOM:

```
SearchInputElement searchElement = querySelector('#q');
DivElement statusElement = querySelector('#status');
DivElement resultsElement = querySelector('#results');
```

The `querySelector()` method uses a selector string that identifies an element in the DOM. See "Finding elements" on page 82 for more about selectors.

 This code could just use `var` instead of specifying types (SearchInputElement[2] and DivElement[3]) for the elements. Whoever writes the code gets to choose whether to specify types.

Handling Events

The client app uses `onChange.listen()` to register a handler that reacts to user input. Whenever the user presses Enter, the search field fires a change event, and the handler kicks off a search:

```
searchElement.onChange.listen((e) {
  //...Start the search...
});
```

Getting and Setting Properties

The change event handler gets and sets the text in the search field using the `value` property:

```
search(searchElement.value);
searchElement.value = '';
```

---

2. *https://api.dartlang.org/dart_html/SearchInputElement.html*
3. *https://api.dartlang.org/dart_html/DivElement.html*

Adding DOM Elements

Every time the search client receives a result on the WebSocket, the client creates a new div (result) to display it. The client then adds that new div to the "results" div (result sElement):

```
void addResult(String source, String title, String link) {
  var result = new DivElement();
  result.children.add(new HeadingElement.h2()..innerHtml = source);
  result.children.add(
      new AnchorElement(href: link)
      ..innerHtml = title
      ..target = '_blank');
  result.classes.add('result');
  resultsElement.children.add(result);
}
```

This code uses method cascades to avoid creating variables to temporarily hold the new HeadingElement and AnchorElement.

Encoding and Decoding Messages

The dart:convert library's global JSON object lets you encode and decode JSON-formatted messages. JSON is an easy way to provide string message data to WebSockets. Using JSON also gives a bit of structure to the messages and leaves the door open to creating more detailed messages in the future.

The JSON.encode() method converts a Dart object to a JSON-encoded string, and the JSON.decode() method converts a JSON string back into a Dart object.

Here's the code that creates a JSON-encoded search request:

```
var request = {
  'request': 'search',
  'input': input
};
webSocket.send(JSON.encode(request));
```

Here's how the client decodes and processes a JSON response from the server:

```
var json = JSON.decode(data);
var response = json['response'];
switch (response) {
  case 'searchResult':
    addResult(json['source'], json['title'], json['link']);
    break;
  ...
}
```

For more information, see "dart:convert—Decoding and Encoding JSON, UTF-8, and More" on page 96.

Communicating with WebSockets

The search client connects to the WebSocket by calling the WebSocket constructor with the argument 'ws://127.0.0.1:9223/ws'. Then it adds event handlers for open and error events. The open event handler, in turn, registers handlers for message and close events. Here's the relevant code:

```
class Client {
  ...
  WebSocket webSocket;
  ...

  Client() {
    ...
    connect();
  }

  void connect() {
    ...
    webSocket = new WebSocket('ws://${Uri.base.host}:${Uri.base.port}/ws');
    webSocket.onOpen.first.then((_) {
      onConnected();
      webSocket.onClose.first.then((_) {
        print("Connection disconnected to ${webSocket.url}");
        onDisconnected();
      });
      webSocket.onError.first.then((_) {...});
    }
  }

  void onConnected() {
    ...
    webSocket.onMessage.listen((e) {
      handleMessage(e.data);
    });
  }
  ...
}
```

To send a message on the WebSocket connection, the client invokes WebSocket's send() method:

```
webSocket.send(JSON.encode(request));
```

When the client receives a message, it decodes the JSON data (as you saw before) and updates the UI to match:

```
void handleMessage(data) {
  var json = JSON.decode(data);
  var response = json['response'];
  switch (response) {
    case 'searchResult':
      addResult(json['source'], json['title'], json['link']);
```

```
      break;

    case 'searchDone':
      setStatus(resultsElement.children.isEmpty
          ? "$mostRecentSearch: No results found"
          : "$mostRecentSearch: ${resultsElement.children.length} results found");
      break;

    default:
      print("Invalid response: '$response'");
  }
}
```

The Server's Code

The main code for the search server is under the bin directory, in a file named serv
er.dart. It's responsible for serving static files, managing WebSocket connections, and
starting searches.

The code for performing the searches is in a custom library, called search_engine, that's
implemented in files under the lib directory.

Serving Static Files

The search server uses HttpServer (from dart:io), Platform (also from dart:io), and
VirtualDirectory (from the http_server package) to implement a basic web server. Here's
the code that initializes the web server and serves static files:

```
var buildPath = Platform.script.resolve('../build').toFilePath();
...
int port = 9223;

HttpServer.bind(InternetAddress.LOOPBACK_IP_V4, port).then((server) {
  ...
  var router = new Router(server);
  ...
  var virDir = new http_server.VirtualDirectory(buildPath);
  virDir.jailRoot = false;
  virDir.allowDirectoryListing = true;
  virDir.directoryHandler = (dir, request) {
    var indexUri = new Uri.file(dir.path).resolve('index.html');
    virDir.serveFile(new File(indexUri.toFilePath()), request);
  };
  ...
  virDir.serve(router.defaultStream);
  ...
});
```

The call to HttpServer.bind() creates a web server that handles HTTP requests to the
address 127.0.0.1:9223 (also known as localhost:9223).

Once the future returned by bind() completes, the code creates a Router (more about that later) and a VirtualDirectory (virDir). Because packages used by the client are set up using symbolic links pointing outside the root directory, ../build, the jailRoot property of virDir must be false. (By default, symbolic links aren't allowed outside the root directory.) The next line sets allowDirectoryListing to true, allowing the web server to respond to paths that don't include a filename. Next, a custom directory handler overrides the default directory listing code, so that directories display index.html instead of a list of files.

Once the VirtualDirectory is all set up, invoking the serve() method connects vir Dir to a stream of HTTP requests. This stream consists of every HTTP request that the router doesn't handle specially—for example, the stream doesn't include WebSocket connection requests.

Managing WebSocket Connections

The search server uses the Router class from the route package[4] to serve dynamic content. In this app, the main purpose of the router is to filter out upgrade HTTP requests for /ws and to handle them as WebSocket connections. The code uses dart:io's Web-SocketTransformer class to perform the conversion:

```
router.serve('/ws')
  .transform(new WebSocketTransformer())
  .listen(handleWebSocket);
```

Here's the custom handleWebSocket() method, which handles events on the WebSocket:

```
void handleWebSocket(WebSocket webSocket) {
  webSocket
    .map((string) => JSON.decode(string))
    .listen((json) {
      var request = json['request'];
      switch (request) {
        case 'search':
          // ...Kick off searches, and register handlers for results...
          break;
        ...
      }
    }, onError: (error) {...});
}
```

The call to webSocket.map() parses all the messages that the client sends over the Web-Socket, converting each JSON-formatted message into an object. Then, after checking the message format, the handler initiates searches on GitHub and StackOverflow.

---

4. *http://pub.dartlang.org/packages/route*

Here's the code from the 'search' case that starts the searches and handles results as they come in:

```
for (var engine in searchEngines) {
  engine.search(input)
    .listen((result) {
      var response = {
        'response': 'searchResult',
        'source': engine.name,
        'title': result.title,
        'link': result.link
      };
      webSocket.add(JSON.encode(response));
    }, onError: (error) {
      ...
    }, onDone: () {
      done++;
      if (done == searchEngines.length) {
        webSocket.add(JSON.encode({ 'response': 'searchDone' }));
      }
    });
```

Each engine can return up to three results, but the WebSocket handler doesn't wait around for those results. Instead, a listener handles each result as it arrives, constructing a JSON-formatted message and using `webSocket.add()` to forward the result to the client. Once both engines have finished sending any results, the search server sends a 'searchDone' message to the client.

Using Web APIs

The GitHub and StackOverflow searches are implemented in `search()` methods that take an input string and return a stream of SearchResult objects. Here's an example from the GitHub `search()` method:

```
import 'package:http/http.dart' as http_client;
...
Stream<SearchResult> search(String input) {
  var query = {
    'q': 'language:dart $input'
  };
  var searchUri = new Uri.https(
      'api.github.com',
      '/search/repositories',
      query);
  var controller = new StreamController();
  http_client.get(searchUri)
    .then((http_client.Response response) {
      if (response.statusCode != HttpStatus.OK) {
        throw "Bad status code: ${response.statusCode},"
              "message: ${response.reasonPhrase}";
```

```
      }
      var json = JSON.decode(response.body);
      json.putIfAbsent('items', () => []);
      json['items']
        .expand(/* Delete items with empty descriptions. */)
        .take(3)
        .forEach((item) {
          controller.add(new SearchResult(
              item['description'], item['html_url']));
        });
    })
    .catchError(controller.addError)
    .whenComplete(controller.close);
  return controller.stream;
}
```

This method first constructs a search URI, using the Uri.https() constructor from dart:core's Uri class. The third argument is a Map<String, String> that specifies the Uri's query parameters. For example, if the input string is 'polymer', then the URI is this:

```
https://api.github.com/search/repositories?q=language%3Adart+polymer
```

Next, the method creates an instance of StreamController (a class from dart:async) to create and manage the stream of results.

Next comes the search request, using the http package's get() function to send an HTTP GET request to the search URI. The get() function returns a Future<Response>. The then() method registers a handler for the response, catchError() registers an error handler, and whenComplete() registers a cleanup function. At this point, the search() method returns the stream created by StreamController.

Once the response arrives, the response handler decodes it and adds the first three reasonable results to the result stream. If an error occurs, then an error goes in the result stream, causing the search client's onError handler to execute. After either a successful completion or an error, the stream closes and the search client's onDone handler executes.

Implementing a Library

The search server implements a library, named search_engine, that contains all the code for performing searches. The search_engine library is declared in search_en gine.dart, with additional implementation in github_search_engine.dart and stack_overflow_search_engine.dart. Here's the code that sets up the library:

```
// In search_engine.dart:

library search_engine;

import 'dart:async';
```

```
import 'dart:convert' show JSON;
import 'dart:io' show HttpStatus;
import 'package:http/http.dart' as http_client;

part 'github_search_engine.dart';
part 'stack_overflow_search_engine.dart';

...
```

The other files in the library don't have imports. They do, however, have `part` of statements, which let tools and programmers know which library relies on these files:

```
// In github_search_engine.dart and stack_overflow_search_engine.dart:

part of search_engine;

...
```

The implementation of the search_engine library is split as follows:

search_engine.dart

Contains two basic classes, SearchResult and SearchEngine. A SearchResult contains a title and a link. SearchEngine is an abstract class that defines a common API for all search engines: a `name` property and a `search()` method that takes a string argument and returns a Stream<SearchResult>.

github_search_engine.dart

Implements GithubSearchEngine, a SearchEngine subclass that searches GitHub for Dart projects that include the search string.

stack_overflow_search_engine.dart

Implements StackOverflowSearchEngine, a SearchEngine subclass that searches StackOverflow for Dart questions with the search string in the title.

The bulk of the code is in the SearchEngine subclasses.

Logging Messages

The search server uses the logging package[5] to log messages at varying levels of severity. Here's the code from `bin/server.dart` that imports API from the logging package and creates a log:

```
import 'package:logging/logging.dart' show Logger, Level, LogRecord;
...
final Logger log = new Logger('DartiverseSearch');
```

The Logger class has many methods for logging messages at pre-defined levels. Here's an example of logging an informational message, which you might use for debugging:

---

5. *http://pub.dartlang.org/packages/logging*

```
log.info('New WebSocket connection');
```

Here's an example of logging a warning:

```
log.warning("Invalid request: '$request'");
```

By default, the logging package doesn't do anything useful with the log messages. You must configure the logging level and add a handler for the log messages. Here's the code from bin/server.dart that creates and configures the Logger object:

```
final Logger log = new Logger('DartiverseSearch');
...

void main() {
  // Set up logger.
  Logger.root.level = Level.ALL;
  Logger.root.onRecord.listen((LogRecord rec) {
    print('${rec.level.name}: ${rec.time}: ${rec.message}');
  });
  ...
}
```

Setting the level to Level.ALL makes all logging messages appear in the onRecord stream. If you want only warnings to appear, you can set the level to Level.WARNING.

For a list of all the levels and what they mean, see the Level API documentation[6]. See the Logger API documentation[7] for a list of methods that log messages.

What Next?

You've seen how the Dartiverse Search sample uses both server-side and client-side Dart code to implement a web app. It makes use of both built-in libraries and libraries from packages published on pub.dartlang.org.

If you'd like to continue exploring Dartiverse Search, consider improving its user interface or adding another search engine. If you'd like to look at other samples, you can find them in Dart Editor and at *http://dartlang.org/samples*.

Our website has lots more information, including guides and tutorials. It's all at *http://dartlang.org*.

---

6. *https://api.dartlang.org/logging/Level.html*
7. *https://api.dartlang.org/logging/Logger.html*

About the Authors

Kathy Walrath is a technical writer who's worked on docs for Chrome and other developer APIs at Google since 2006. Before that, she worked at Sun, NeXT, and HP. Back when the Web was young, she wrote the first doc to help developers write Java applets. She also co-created *The Java Tutorial* and maintained it for a very long time.

Seth Ladd is a Developer Advocate with the Chrome team. He is a conference organizer (Aloha on Rails, New Game) and author (*Expert Spring MVC and Web Flow* [Apress]), helped publish Angry Birds for the Web, and is a big fan of HTML5 and the modern Web.

Have it your way.

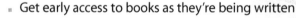

Get even more for your money.

Join the O'Reilly Community, and register the O'Reilly books you own. It's free, and you'll get:

- $4.99 ebook upgrade offer
- 40% upgrade offer on O'Reilly print books
- Membership discounts on books and events
- Free lifetime updates to ebooks and videos
- Multiple ebook formats, DRM FREE
- Participation in the O'Reilly community
- Newsletters
- Account management
- 100% Satisfaction Guarantee

Signing up is easy:

1. **Go to: oreilly.com/go/register**
2. **Create an O'Reilly login.**
3. **Provide your address.**
4. **Register your books.**

Note: English-language books only

To order books online:
oreilly.com/store

For questions about products or an order:
orders@oreilly.com

To sign up to get topic-specific email announcements and/or news about upcoming books, conferences, special offers, and new technologies:
elists@oreilly.com

For technical questions about book content:
booktech@oreilly.com

To submit new book proposals to our editors:
proposals@oreilly.com

O'Reilly books are available in multiple DRM-free ebook formats. For more information:
oreilly.com/ebooks

O'REILLY®

Spreading the knowledge of innovators   oreilly.com

Ingram Content Group UK Ltd.
Milton Keynes UK
UKHW030615080323
418199UK00007B/368